GUARD YOUR HEART

Dr. Gary and Barbara
Rosberg

TYNDALE HOUSE PUBLISHERS, INC.
WHEATON, ILLINOIS

Visit Tyndale's exciting Web site at www.tyndale.com

Guard Your Heart

Copyright © 2003 by Gary and Barbara Rosberg. All rights reserved.

Author photo copyright © 2002 by Thomas and Bruce Photography. All rights reserved.

Published in association with the literary agency of Alive Communications, Inc., 7680 Goddard Street, Suite 200, Colorado Springs, CO 80920.

The names and some of the details in the illustrations used in this book have been changed to protect the privacy of the people who shared their stories with us.

This book is adapted from *Guard Your Heart,* originally written as a book for men. Copyright © 2001 by Gary Rosberg. Used by permission of Tyndale House Publishers, Inc., Wheaton, Illinois 60189. All rights reserved.

Designed by Julie Chen

Edited by Lynn Vanderzalm

Unless otherwise indicated, all Scripture quotations are taken from the *Holy Bible,* New Living Translation, copyright © 1996. Used by permission of Tyndale House Publishers, Inc., Wheaton, Illinois 60189. All rights reserved.

Scripture quotations marked NIV are taken from the *Holy Bible,* New International Version®. NIV®. Copyright © 1973, 1978, 1984 by International Bible Society. Used by permission of Zondervan Publishing House. All rights reserved.

Library of Congress Cataloging-in-Publication Data

Rosberg, Gary, date.
   Guard your heart / Gary and Barbara Rosberg.
     p. cm.
Includes bibliographical references.
   ISBN 0-8423-5732-7 (SC)
   1. Husbands—Religious life. 2. Wives—Religious life. 3. Married people—Religious life.
4. Marriage—Religious aspects—Christianity. I. Rosberg, Barbara. II. Title.
BV4846.R67 2003
248.8′44—dc21   2002154867

Printed in the United States of America

08   07   06   05   04   03
8   7   6   5   4   3   2   1

This book is dedicated personally

to Team Tyndale—

Ron Beers, Ken Petersen,

Lynn Vanderzalm, Ed Stewart, and Dave Bellis—

and collectively

to the entire publishing team at Tyndale House.

We count it a joy to partner with you in the campaign to

divorce-proof America's marriages.

CONTENTS

Acknowledgments

This book is dedicated to Team Tyndale. We call them Team Tyndale because Tyndale House Publishers has partnered with our ministry, America's Family Coaches, to publish resources to help take back the American family for the cause of Jesus Christ. Tyndale House is far more than a publisher to us; the people at Tyndale are our friends and colaborers in ministry. To a person—from copy editors to graphic designers, from administrative assistants to marketing managers—this publishing house is serving Jesus Christ with excellence and honor. Therefore, it is *our honor* to honor Team Tyndale. Dr. Ken Taylor, your passion is being carried to the next generation with your son, Mark Taylor, and his team. Thank you for equipping us to fight the good fight with you. Guard your hearts, friends.

We also want to acknowledge the men of CrossTrainers. For thirteen years I (Gary) have had the joy of ministering to you each Wednesday, consistently reminding you of Solomon's words in Proverbs 4:23: "Guard your heart, for it is the wellspring of life" (NIV). Stay the course, men. Let's finish the race with integrity, together, serving our wives, children, and grandchildren with honor and integrity. Thank you for equipping us to minister to families at home and across the country. Guard your hearts, friends.

Thanks to our board of directors (Jerry Foster, Steve Durick, Greg Webster, Marcia Bergren, and George Tracey) and ministry team at America's Family Coaches. Your belief in this campaign and what we have been called to is changing all of our lives. Your sacrifice, service, and passion are constant reminders to us that we have surrounded ourselves with the *best of the best* in America. We tip our hats to you! Guard your hearts, friends.

Thank you also, to Salem Radio Network. Greg Anderson, you are equipping us through *America's Family Coaches . . . LIVE!* to expand the message of this book and campaign throughout America on a daily basis. Your belief and partnership with us humbles us. God is using you! Your team, especially Charles Mefferd, is top-notch. Guard your hearts, friends.

And finally, and most intimately, thanks to our children and grandson. If we don't succeed at home, then this entire campaign will falter. Thank you for your unfailing love, grace, and belief. We are the most fulfilled parents and grandparents in America. Sarah and Scott, guard your hearts. Missy, guard your heart. Mason, guard your heart. We promise to finish strong, together, and guard *our* hearts. We love you!

Dear friend,

The book in your hands is a vital part of a campaign to Divorce-Proof America's Marriages. Couples across this nation—from Boston to Los Angeles, from Miami to Seattle—are joining together to divorce-proof their marriages. They are taking a stand *for* healthy, growing, lifetime marriages and *against* the looming threat of divorce.

Why now?

If we don't do it *now,* then when?

If we don't start *here*—with our family and yours—then where?

If we don't do it *together,* who will?

We believe that if we fail to address divorce now, the next generation of marriages will be lost. We must catch the vision for divorce-proof marriages and push back the threat of divorce as far as our influence can reach. We want to join you not only in proactively protecting your own marriage but in helping divorce-proof the marriage of every couple you know.

As we go to battle together for the cause of the Christian home, we will pay a price. We have a powerful enemy in this endeavor. The apostle Peter warns, "Be careful! Watch out for attacks from the Devil, your great enemy. He prowls around like a roaring lion, looking for some victim to devour" (1 Peter 5:8).

You and your marriage are the devil's intended victims. Since a divorce-proof marriage is high on God's priority list, you can know that such marriages are also at the top of the enemy's hit list. Satan would like nothing better than to discourage you, debilitate your marriage, and add another crippled or broken family to his ledger. That is why we are asserting that your marriage and family *are* your ministry.

Let us proclaim together loudly and clearly: Divorce will stop—and stop *now*. Starting in our home and in yours, let's draw a line in the sand and tell anyone with ears to hear, "As for me and my family, we will serve the Lord" (Joshua 24:15). Let's agree to pull out all the stops in order to build biblical homes—for the sake of our marriages, for the sake of the next generation, and for the cause of Jesus Christ.

But it doesn't stop there. If you—as a couple, a pastor, a small-group leader, an adult Sunday school teacher—share these principles with other couples and families you care about, you will become part of God's work to change the face of marriage in our country. (For additional resources, as well as ideas about how to start a small group in your community, please see the appendix.)

How does *Guard Your Heart* fit into the campaign? We believe that our marriages face lots of temptations—some obvious, some subtle. If we do not guard our hearts and the hearts of our spouses, we will be at risk for sliding toward disconnection, discord, and possibly emotional divorce. Guarding love—the kind of love that protects from threats and helps spouses feel safe and secure—is a critical part of divorce-proofing any marriage. This book and the companion *Guarding Love* workbook will help you develop and practice guarding love, one of the six different kinds of love outlined in our campaign book, *Divorce-Proof Your Marriage.*

We hope you catch the vision for divorce-proofing your marriage—and the marriages of people you know. It's a campaign worth investing in!

Your friends,
Gary and Barb Rosberg

Part One

THE ASSAULT ON YOUR MARRIAGE

Chapter One

YOUR MARRIAGE: A TARGET

İT WAS A MUGGY TUESDAY MORNING, A SUBTLE SIGNAL THAT summer in Iowa wasn't quite over. I rose early, kissed Barb good-bye, and drove out to the new campus of the large, growing West Des Moines church where we are members. Barb and I were in the final stages of preparation for the kickoff of our national Divorce-Proofing America's Marriages campaign. The launch would take place in only a few days with our first major conference right here in our home church.

The purpose of that early morning meeting was to pray with the church's pastors and elders about the upcoming conference. We were all too aware that the marriages and families in our church were under attack. Satan is just as active in West Des Moines as he is in your community, attempting to damage lives, destroy marriages, and divide families. We were gathering that Tuesday morning as part of a determined counteroffensive. As church leaders, we were drawing a line in the sand to say corporately, "No more, not here. As for me and my house, we will serve the Lord."

I arrived early and walked through the sanctuary, praying over every seat, anticipating what God would do in the lives of the approximately eleven hundred people who would attend the conference. By God's grace, we were going to take back some territory that the enemy had wrongfully claimed as his own. As I prayed, I sensed a rekindling of the call God had placed on Barb's heart and mine: to lay down our lives in ministry for the families of America. Faith rose within me. I knew God was ready to do great things in the marriages and families of our city and around the country.

I had just completed my sanctuary prayer walk and had begun praying with the elders when one of the elders who had left the church early hurried back into the sanctuary. He had received a call on his cell phone and had returned to relay the message to us in somber tones. "My wife says there's been a plane crash in New York City. We need to turn on the TV. They're saying America is under attack."

It was Tuesday morning, September 11, 2001—a date we all refer to today simply as 9/11. Like Barb and me, you will never forget where you were that morning.

I joined our pastors and elders around a television set in the church office. We watched in numb shock as the sky around the first World Trade Center tower filled with smoke. Then a jetliner slammed into the second tower, exploding into a ball of flames—right before our eyes. I was horrified and grief-stricken, realizing that hundreds of people had died in that incident alone.

News coverage cut away to the Pentagon in Washington, D.C., and the smoldering remains of a third airplane crash. Soon there was news of another crash outside Pittsburgh, Pennsylvania, a crash that perhaps was connected to the others. It was a terrorist attack, everyone on TV now said. Where would they strike next? We prayed together as a group, then we rushed out to the parking lot and headed home to our families.

Barb had been watching television when the whole event unfolded before her eyes on the screen. When I got home, we called our two grown daughters to comfort them and reassure them. Then we watched in horror as the first and then the second tower collapsed. The early projections were staggering: thousands of innocent people killed in the attack. What kind of people were behind such a diabolical act?

We were awestruck by the irony. At the same time I was praying against the attack on the families in our church, terrorists were unleashing the most devastating peacetime attack on the United States in its history. The spiritual battle in West Des Moines, Iowa, was only a microcosm of what was happening across our great country. The reality burned into our hearts: We are in a spiritual conflict with eternal ramifications, and we dare not become complacent.

FAIR WARNING

If we learned anything from 9/11, we learned that the world is not always a safe place. As pleasant and positive as most people are, there are also bad people out there, people who—for whatever twisted reason—are out to hurt instead of help, to wound instead of welcome. If we forget this reality or become too complacent in a sense of comfort and safety—*wham!*—someone with evil intent will take advantage of us. It happened one fall morning in New York City, rural Pennsylvania, and Washington, D.C. It happens every day in every corner of our fallen world. It's not only good common sense; it's a code to live by: be careful, be alert—or be sorry.

The battles against terrorism and other destructive influences in the physical world are not even half the story. We know that we are also in a spiritual battle. God's archenemy, Satan, is the ultimate terrorist, intent on bringing down anything God chooses and cherishes. The enemy works from the inside out, assaulting our minds and hearts, tempting us to sins of commission and omission, tantalizing us to compromise our obedience to Christ. We must be constantly on guard against this scheming devil whose mission is to "steal and kill and destroy" (John 10:10).

No wonder Jesus offered warning after warning during his earthly ministry. Be on your guard, he said, against hypocrisy (Matthew 16:6-12), against greed (Luke 12:15), against persecution from others (Matthew 10:17), against false teaching (Mark 13:22-23), and against spiritual laziness and being unprepared for the Lord's return (Mark 13:32-37). "Be careful," he said in Luke 21:34, "or your hearts will be weighed down with dissipation [another word for wild living], drunkenness and the anxieties of life [wildness may not be your problem, but maybe worry is]" (NIV).

The same caution echoes throughout the Scriptures. Take note and let each warning sink in:

⊕ "Be careful to do what the Lord your God has commanded you." (Deuteronomy 5:32, NIV)

⊕ "Be careful that you do not forget the Lord." (Deuteronomy 6:12, NIV)

⊕ "Be careful to obey all that is written in the Book of the Law of Moses." (Joshua 23:6, NIV)

⊕ "I am the Lord your God; . . . be careful to keep my laws." (Ezekiel 20:19, NIV)

⊕ "Give careful thought to your ways." (Haggai 1:5, NIV)

⊕ "Be careful to do what is right." (Romans 12:17, NIV)

⊕ "Be careful that you don't fall!" (1 Corinthians 10:12, NIV)

⊕ "Be very careful, then, how you live." (Ephesians 5:15, NIV)

⊕ "Be careful that none of you be found to have fallen short." (Hebrews 4:1, NIV)

Be careful. Watch out. Be on guard. Because if you don't get hit today, you can bet you will be hit tomorrow or the day after. This is no action-adventure movie we're living in; it really is a hazardous and dangerous world out there.

FAMILIES UNDER ATTACK

The warnings of Scripture are very relevant to our marriages and families. You and your spouse, along with your children, are near the top of the enemy's hit list. Your marriage is God's creation; your family is God's joy. So Satan is working hard to destroy your family relationship, demoralize you, and discredit your witness. He wants to isolate you from each other, from the Lord, and from other Christian families.

That's why we need the Lord—as individuals, couples, and families. That's why we need each other as husbands and wives. And that's why we need other believers around us: fellow church members, a Bible study group, a home fellowship group, or an accountability group. As a spouse and parent, you need someone to watch your back, monitor your blind spots, and walk beside you over the long haul. It's nearly impossible to guard your heart, your marriage, and your family alone.

For this very reason, our Divorce-Proofing America's Marriages campaign challenges couples to band together to study God's Word and apply biblically based divorce-proofing principles to their relationships. The enemy of our souls is not the kind of enemy you want to tackle one-on-one. When the crunch comes, you want other couples to stand with you and battle with you for your marriage and family.

The apostle Paul must have been thinking about these kinds of relationships when he wrote a few words to his friend and protégé Timothy. The old missionary soldier wrote, "I have fought a good fight, I have finished the race, and I have remained faithful" (2 Timothy 4:7). When you are nearing the end of your life, wouldn't you as a couple love to send a letter to your grown children, your grandchildren, and your dearest Christian friends and boldly say something like that? "It's been a bloody fight against the enemies of our relationship, but we have battled to the end. It's been a tough race, but we're going to cross the finish line as winners. It's been a constant battle to keep our marriage on track, but here we are, still in one piece, and still together, ready to face our Lord."

Paul was alone sometimes during his ministry, but even then he depended on the friends who sustained him in vulnerable moments. Timothy was Paul's friend through ups and downs, hot and cold, thick and thin. Who are your friends? What other couples are praying for you as husband and wife? Who is checking in on you from time to time? If you don't have at least one or two other Christian couples who are standing with you prayerfully, you are particularly vulnerable to attack. A hungry lion in search of dinner watches for prey who have been separated from the safety of the herd. Similarly, Satan stalks about like a ravenous lion, looking for easy pickings. He knows that you are easier to bring down when you have no one to support you and protect you.

Behind every attack on your marriage and family is the master terrorist, Satan. Whatever strategy he may use to come after you, he always goes for the heart. That's why we need to guard our hearts. Because just when we begin to relax our guard, thinking our marriage is invulnerable to attack, he swoops in and nails us. As you will see shortly, if the enemy can get to your heart and the heart of your marriage, he has a good chance of bringing you down.

WHY LISTEN TO US?

Why should you listen to us? Why do Barb and I have anything to tell you about marriages under attack, about guarding against the enemy of your heart, your marriage, and your family? Is it because I have a degree in counseling? No. My degree has equipped me to better understand the dynamics of marriage and family relationships, but the degree isn't enough to give us credibility to discuss the importance of guarding against attack.

Should you listen to us because Barb and I head a national ministry called America's Family Coaches, conduct marriage conferences around the country, and speak to hundreds of thousands of radio listeners every day on our live call-in program? No. Even though the ministry God has called us to has given us a broad platform to help men and women divorce-proof their families, it also isn't enough to give us credibility to say what needs to be said about guarding your heart.

Our number one qualification for helping you take a stand against the enemy of your marriage and family is that we've been there. We know what it means to be attacked. We came to understand the serious potential of unguarded hearts early in our marriage. Barb and I took a major hit that had the potential of derailing everything God had in store for us as individuals, a couple, and parents—and the attack would have hit our two beautiful daughters, Sarah and Missy, as well. We know that the heart of a Christian couple is vulnerable and in danger of a sinister and crippling attack because we lived through a subtle attack that slowly, almost imperceptibly, drew us apart emotionally. We tell the story in greater detail in our book *Divorce-Proof Your Marriage,* but let us summarize it here.

NAILED TO THE WALL BY A FIVE-YEAR-OLD

While I was completing my doctoral program, life was rather hectic for us. I was holding down a full-time job, studying most nights at the university library, and trying to be a good husband and father. And I thought I was doing a pretty decent job of it. Then one day little five-year-old Sarah brought me a picture she had drawn. "Daddy," she said, "look at the picture I drew of our family. Do you like it?"

As I studied the colorful crayon family portrait, I noticed an obvious omission. She had drawn herself, her mommy, and her sister, Missy. Even our dog, Katie, was there. But I was no-where in the picture.

Pointing to her artwork, I inquired, "Sarah, where's Daddy?"

"Oh," she replied, "you're at the library."

Sarah's simple picture and explanation stunned me. It was the same kind of feeling I had seeing those airplanes hit the World Trade Center towers. I was immediately aware that something was very wrong, that I had been blind to an evil plot against my marriage and family. That day, suddenly, it exploded in my face. Our daughter saw me in the house nearly every day, but somehow she didn't see me as part of her family.

Staring at the picture, I was deeply shaken. Here I was, on the verge of becoming a professional Christian family coun-selor, and my own family relationship was in crisis. But instead of responding to Sarah and the situation at that time, I shut down emotionally and did nothing—mostly because I hadn't a clue about what to do.

I taped Sarah's picture to the dining room wall where Barb would see it. I didn't have the courage to show it to her myself. She saw it but said nothing to me. I wanted to talk to her about my extended absence from the family, but I didn't know what to say. I was in agony.

At the same time, Barb was also struggling. She had been as excited about my pursuing my doctorate as I was. We went into the grueling program with eyes wide open and completely in agreement. But as I became more and more of an absentee husband and father, she was tired and hurting—for good reason. I wasn't pulling my weight as a husband and father. Barb had always been optimistic, but even that was changing. She cried more often, growing more resentful toward my schooling, complaining more about my absence. Then she began to shut down emotionally. Our marriage was clearly under attack on both sides.

One night, weeks after Sarah showed me her picture, I crawled into bed and asked Barb a question. The lights were out, and I wasn't even sure she was awake. I said, "Did you see the family picture that Sarah drew?"

"Yes," she whispered.

Then I posed a simple, childlike question: "Barb, may I come home?"

I didn't have to explain. Barb understood. She too had sensed that I was no longer with her as I used to be. My body ate and slept at home, but my heart was far away from the very people I claimed to hold dearest. That night I acutely felt the loneliness Barb and our girls had been feeling for months and perhaps years. I wanted to come home, but I wondered if I was welcome anymore.

After a brief pause, Barb answered. "Yes, Gary, I want you to come home. I love you. The girls love you. But no one knows you anymore."

I loved my wife and two daughters dearly. And the things I was doing—the work, the studying, everything—I considered to be for them. But Barb's comment, "No one knows you anymore," emphasized how our family relationship had deteriorated right before our eyes. Her words revealed that our marriage and family life had been sabotaged.

The good news is that we heeded our wake-up call, made some critical changes in our relationship, and survived the assault. Our marriage has grown richer and deeper in the twenty-plus years since then. But the experience has underscored to us that any marriage—even a good Christian marriage like ours and perhaps yours—is vulnerable to attack. We must learn to guard our hearts.

It Was Right in Front of Us, but We Didn't See It

In the months following 9/11, the irony became painfully clear. The Twin Towers and the Pentagon were not hit by missiles launched by an enemy on the other side of the globe. The terrorists who carried out the attack on America had been living among us for months. These murderers plotted this horrible attack right under our noses. They were here as welcome visitors. They were living in our own cities and towns. They learned to fly commercial jets at our flight schools. They boarded aircraft that morning with tickets we sold to them. They carried knives and box cutters onto those planes through our own security systems. The 9/11 attack on America was an inside job. We just didn't see it—until it was too late.

That's what happened to Barb and me. The assault on our marriage didn't come from the outside. There wasn't "another woman" or "another man" in the picture. I wasn't lured away from devotion to my family by pornography. Barb wasn't distracted from me by sordid romance novels or soap operas. We had our defense systems in place for these kinds of obvious attacks. In the meantime, we were just cruising through life, unaware that our hearts were being seduced by the frantic lifestyle we had chosen. It was an inside job; we had been blinded by the fog around us, and we had left our hearts unguarded.

CUTTING THROUGH THE FOG

Where is the fog in your life? Has a gray gloom drifted into your marriage? Has it chilled your closeness with your spouse? If someone were to ask you, "How's your marriage doing?" would you be tempted to say, "It's okay," while uncomfortably aware that it is not as okay as it should be? Is a subtle haze of loneliness hanging between you and your spouse, and between the two of you and your children?

Or perhaps there is an all-out rebellion in your home. Your kids scream out or act out trying to get your attention. Your spouse goes from whispering, to shouting, to silence, sometimes concluding in isolation that the person he or she married is lost somewhere. And you wonder when the fog rolled in. When did your dream marriage begin to deteriorate?

Maybe you don't seek God's presence and purpose in your marriage as you used to. You have become distracted from the most important relationships in your life. You have become self-absorbed. You forget to look up to the Father who loves you. You forget to consider the Savior who died and rose for you, and the Holy Spirit who is present to empower you. God is right there in your life and in your marriage, but you can't see him. You are in some kind of fog.

We can tell you from our own experience that your hearts are under siege. The enemy wants to blanket you with a fog of complacency, apathy, or resignation, convince you that your marriage is good enough when it really hasn't been that good for some time now. It may be an okay marriage, but it is far from the dream of marriage you two started out with.

God has any number of means at his disposal to slice through the haze and get your attention. He wants to alert you to the terrorist attack on your marriage and family before the big bomb goes off—an affair, a threat of separation or divorce, a runaway child, or any number of other threats. This book may be one way God is trying to wake you to the reality that your hearts are vulnerable and in danger. Will you let him get your attention?

After God finally got my attention—with my daughter's family portrait—it was a couple of years before I finally celebrated being home. It was a banner day for me as the three most important people in my life announced they had a gift for me. I smiled broadly—until our younger daughter, then five-year-old Missy, said it was a "drawing of our family." My heart thumped hard in my chest, remembering the shock of a previous family portrait. But I knew I had to look at Missy's picture.

I held my breath as my eyes scanned the picture. There was Barb with her yellow hair. There were Sarah and Missy and Katie the dog and a big sun smiling down from the sky. And there was a tall guy with a mustache, standing smack in the middle of his family. Daddy was back in the picture, back where I belonged.

Missy's family picture still hangs in my office. Each day as Barb and I work with hurting families needing hope, we have that portrait nearby. It's a reminder to us that God can do miracles in marriages that are under siege. He did it for us, and he can do it for you.

You Can Win the Battle

As you come to grips with the reality of the assault on your marriage and family, you may be wondering, "Can I win this battle?" God's answer is, "Yes—with me, you can." It doesn't matter where you are in your relationship with your spouse and your children, God knows your heart. He knows where you are vulnerable, where the enemy has aimed his terror, and what to do about it. He knows if your heart is broken or out of tune with him or with your family members. He knows your hidden strengths and your all-too-obvious weaknesses.

He knows you. He knows exactly what you need, and he's there, twenty-four hours a day, to listen, respond, and give direction. Call on him. You need him. He's challenging you to guard your heart, and he will give you the willpower to do it and the firepower you need to resist Satan's attempts to derail your marriage.

You may be saying at this point, "Wait a minute! I'm a lover, not a fighter. Our marriage may not be perfect, but it's okay most of the time. Why would I want to stir up a hornet's nest by going into battle for a better marriage?"

It all has to do with your legacy. As the apostle Paul wrote to his friends in Corinth, each of us is composing a letter with our lives, a letter that others around us—and those who come after us—will read (see 2 Corinthians 3:2). It's your life story, your legacy. What do you want your story to reveal about you? How do you want to be remembered as a husband, wife, or parent? What do you want to say to the world—and more specifically, to your children and grandchildren—about love and marriage? Will anybody learn what God's idea of marriage is all about from your example?

Solomon said, "The memory of the righteous will be a blessing" (Proverbs 10:7, NIV). Will future generations look back at how you and your spouse lived out your relationship and say, "What a blessing!"? You get to decide what your life and your marriage will say to others. You can coast along with an okay marriage, doing the best you can. Or you can draw a line in the sand and say to the enemy, "No more. Our marriage and family will be shaped by God's truth, love, and grace in our lives, not your terrorism." Your choice will dictate the legacy you leave behind.

Several years ago, a dear friend of mine named Henry Oursler drew a simple diagram for me on the back of a napkin as we ate dinner together. The implications of his picture are so vast that I have only begun to deal with them. I have not looked at my life in the same way since. The psalmist David once prayed, "Lord, remind me how brief my time on earth will be. Remind me that my days are numbered, and that my life is fleeing away" (Psalm 39:4). In answer to that prayer, perhaps God sent a good friend to show David the same diagram Henry showed me.

On the napkin, Henry drew a line like the one below. This line represents your life. The arrowhead on one end signifies that your life will go on for eternity. And on the other end you will see five dots. The first dot represents your birth. The second dot represents meeting your spouse. The third is for your marriage. The fourth stands for the arrival of your children. And the fifth dot is the day you will die. You may have more dots, signifying a previous marriage, or fewer dots, if you have no children. But the basic principle is the same.

See how closely the dots are bunched and how long the line is in comparison? If this illustration were accurate, of course, we couldn't even get it on a sheet of paper. The dots would be infinitesimally microscopic, and the line representing eternity would stretch beyond your imagination and comprehension.

This diagram crudely pictures how God views our lives from his eternal perspective. He is the One who gives us the line, a life that will last for eternity. So, in his view, the line—not the dots—is the more significant part of our existence. We tend to make the dots bigger than life. In actuality, many of us live for the dots, for our brief time here on earth.

How about you? Would you rather live for the dots or for the line? Which makes more sense in light of eternity?

The diagram also reminds us that we have a *very short* amount of time on this earth to impact the lives of our spouses and children and create our legacy. This reality should leave all of us with a sense of urgency. The enemy is out to lull us into complacency and lethargy. But this is no time to tread water, to settle for mediocre relationships with the dearest people in our lives. It's time to dig in our heels, stand guard over our hearts, and take back our marriages for the cause of Christ and for the sake of the next generation.

THE SOURCE OF YOUR STORY

If you are like Barb and me, you desire to have a greater impact as a husband or wife and parent than you have had to this point. You want to be remembered as a man or woman who was sold out to loving and nurturing your spouse. You want to be remembered by your children as being lovingly and actively involved in their lives. You want your friends, your coworkers, your neighbors, your fellow church members, and anyone else within the sphere of your influence to note you as someone with three crystal clear priorities:

- A loving commitment to Christ
- A loving commitment to your spouse
- A loving commitment to your children

Where does this kind of legacy come from? Barb and I believe the secret is found in the instruction given long ago by a father to his son. In one of those rare moments when two souls lock together and all else fades from awareness, this concerned dad looked into his boy's eyes and said these words: "Above all else, guard your heart, for it affects everything you do" (Proverbs 4:23). King Solomon admonishes us to guard our hearts well, because our hearts are the source of our life story, our legacy.

These words are just as true as when Solomon, led by the Holy Spirit, wrote them down. What is in your heart today and tomorrow will dictate not only what you do with those five closely bunched dots representing your life but also how others will see you. What is in your heart tells the story of who you really are.

It boils down to this: We need a plan for erecting strong boundaries around our hearts if we are going to protect them from invasion, contamination, and destruction at the hands of our enemy. We need to be on the alert, ready to live without regrets. We don't want to waste our short time on earth pursuing dead ends, wrong turns, and aimless detours. We want a life that makes sense, a life that points toward a destiny beyond time. We desire a marriage and family relationship that, on close inspection, may reveal plenty of mistakes but that is also rich with repentance, forgiveness, and grace.

Is this your heart's desire as a husband or wife? If so, Barb and I want to coach you on how to guard your hearts and create a legacy worth remembering in your marriage and family. We call it *guarding love*. As you learn to guard your heart and the hearts of your spouse and children, you will begin to recapture your marriage dream and to create a legacy that will enrich countless marriages and families around you. So let's get started on the journey of guarding the love of our homes.

Guarding love is one of six key facets of love you need to divorce-proof your marriage. For more information on our Divorce-Proofing America's Marriages campaign, including important resources on other elements of a divorce-proof marriage, see the appendix.

Chapter Two

THE HEART OF THE MATTER

Gary and I were amazed at the story. It shouldn't have happened. It *couldn't* have happened. Yet it did. It was outrageous, implausible, unthinkable. If anyone had dared write it into a Hollywood movie script, the writer would have been laughed right out of the studio. But there it was on page one of the morning papers. On May 29, 1987, a nineteen-year-old West German computer analyst landed his single-engine Cessna in Moscow's Red Square. He stepped out of the plane, smiled at the stunned crowd, and coolly began signing autographs.

The pilot was Mathias Rust, from Hamburg. He had navigated the Cessna 172 to Moscow from Helsinki, Finland, in an unauthorized flight over four hundred miles of the most heavily guarded airspace in the world. Shadowed at intervals by Soviet fighter planes, Rust flew on and on, unchallenged and unscathed. He penetrated the impenetrable. The protection of the former "evil empire's" sprawling frontiers had broken down in a shocking way.

The irony was unmistakable. On the very day the Soviets were celebrating "Border Guards Day," they failed to guard their borders. If Rust had been a cruise missile instead of a young man on a joyride, Moscow might have been reduced to ruins.

At about seven-thirty in the evening, after a sixteen-hour flight, Rust approached Red Square from the south. Muscovites and tourists strolling through the great cobbled plaza looked up to see a little Cessna buzzing Lenin's tomb, then barely clearing the red brick walls of the Kremlin before finally touching down. Rust taxied to within a few feet of the Kremlin wall, just behind the onion-domed St. Basil's Cathedral. The iron heart of world communism had become a landing strip for an amateur pilot with peach fuzz on his chin.

After coming to a stop, Rust jumped out of the plane in a jaunty red flight suit and cheerfully began greeting bystanders while authorities tried to figure out what to do. It seems the Soviet law had no precedent for dealing with a foreign teenager who lands an airplane in Red Square.

"Something this unusual does not happen every day," said one Muscovite who saw the pilot step from his craft.

A Western diplomat in Moscow had a different slant on Rust's flight: "This puts a hole right through one of the great myths of this place, the myth of invincibility and impenetrability."

A Soviet official put it more bluntly: "There are going to be more than red faces among the military over this."

The official was right. Before the next day dawned, Communist Party leader Mikhail Gorbachev sacked seventy-five-year-old Defense Minister Sergei Sokolov. Several weeks later, the novice pilot on his first cross-country solo flight was sentenced to four years in a Soviet labor camp.

Why did Rust do it? He insisted he was "trying to deliver a message of peace." Whatever his reason, he became an immediate celebrity and a new German folk hero. What was next? If a single West German citizen could defy the Kremlin's vaunted defense network, how long could the Berlin Wall stand?

Gary and I can't help thinking about Mr. Rust's incredible feat when we consider Solomon's sobering words in Proverbs

4:23: "Above all else, guard your heart, for it is the wellspring of life" (NIV). You and your spouse may think your hearts are well guarded. You may think your defenses are all in place. You may confidently assume you could never fall to an extramarital affair or a heartbreaking divorce. But on the very day you may celebrate "Border Guards Day" in your hearts, you may be in the most danger of penetration. That's the day your heart could become Satan's landing strip.

We heard a true story about a drowning at a swimming pool in New Orleans. They found the body at the bottom of a pool. A tragedy, yes. But what made it worse was that the man drowned in the middle of a lifeguard convention! In the presence of hundreds of trained, tanned, and athletic lifeguards, someone floundered and drowned. That pool should have been the safest pool in America that day, but one unguarded person paid the ultimate price.

It can be costly to celebrate a victory too early. We cannot afford to let down our guard, thinking we will enjoy clear, unimpeded sailing in our marriages. There are too many dangers out there for us to be complacent and unwary. Gary and I are not alarmists, and we don't want you to feel paranoid. We all face many temptations to impurity, many distractions triggered by our human nature, and many traps set for us by the enemy of our souls. And these attacks are aimed at destroying you and your marriage.

You have all the resources you need in Christ, God's Word, and the Holy Spirit to withstand this relentless assault. But you must take up a defensive position. You must learn to guard your heart. You must equip your closest relationships with a guarding love that will divorce-proof your marriage and family. Gary is going to explore several key statements from Proverbs 4:23 that provide a solid biblical foundation for guarding your heart.

ON GUARD

Barb and I don't pretend to be Hebrew scholars, but we want to focus on a few important elements of Solomon's wise words that will help cement their truth to our lives and family relationships.

"Above All Else"

Solomon really wants our attention, doesn't he? The phrase *above all else* sounds as if we're getting to bottom-line, rock-solid essentials. Think of the people in your life who might say something like *above all else*:

- Your dad stands next to you by the station wagon as he drops you off for your first day of college. Mom has already hugged you and now sits in the car, dabbing her eyes with a tissue. Dad gives you a long, final embrace. He's about to cut some parental strings, but before he does, he looks you straight in the eyes and says, "Just before we go, I have something very important to tell you. Above all else, remember . . ."

- Your grandmother is lying on her deathbed, and you go to say good-bye. A familiar smile crosses her face when she sees you. It's hard for her to speak, but you can tell she has something to say to you. These will be her last words to you in this life. The whisper is faint, but you don't want to miss a syllable. You lean close to her face, and she whispers in your ear, "My dear, above all else . . ."

- Your pastor is concluding one of the most life-changing sermons you have ever heard. It has been a masterful exposition and application of God's Word. The life of the congregation will be forever altered by this Spirit-inspired message. You lean in close as he comes to his final point. "Brothers and sisters, if you forget everything else I've said today, above all else, you must remember . . ."

Whenever we hear words like these, we know we are getting to the core of the message. It's the moment of truth. The phrase *above all else* says that with everything in our sights, this is the thing to focus on.

Can you imagine sitting by the bedside of Solomon, the wisest man in the world, and having him say to you, "I've told you many things in our life together. I've seen it all, owned it all, and experienced it all. So lean close, my child, and let me give you the essence of everything. Here's all you need to know: Above all else . . ."?

Do you get the idea that the words to follow will be among the most important you may ever hear, words that will serve as a major cornerstone for your life? That's just what Solomon is trying to convey as he begins this key verse.

"Guard"

In the original language, the underlying meaning for the word *guard* suggests exercising great care over something. Do you remember the special care you gave to something of value to you? Maybe it was your first new car. You were so proud of it: no scratches, lots of zeros on the odometer, a heady new-car smell, and no McDonald's wrappers or petrified French fries under the seats. You would go out to the garage at night just to look at it and walk slowly around it, maybe giving it a gentle little pat on the taillight.

Or maybe you remember giving extra special care to your first infant. You carried that baby with gentle hands, as if the slightest bump or jiggle would cause him or her great pain. And at night you found yourself creeping into the nursery several times to check on that little bundle. As you gazed at your child in the soft glow of the night-light, you realized that God had allowed you to be part of a miracle. You couldn't be too careful handling that marvel of creation.

When you care deeply about something, you exercise great care over it. When you care deeply about someone, you exercise great care over that person. Solomon says we need to exercise that kind of care over our hearts.

The word *guard* in this verse also means to stand watch over, as a sentry watchfully guards a military encampment against possible enemies or invasion. When Solomon tells us to guard our hearts, he instructs us to be alert and watchful, ready to protect and defend against the enemy.

Put these two pictures together, and here's what you have: exercising great care over our hearts and defending them from harm. If you fail to guard your heart in these ways, you can be easily deceived, captured, and plundered.

"Your Heart"

The heart is the very core of who we are. It speaks to us when we turn off the lights, lay our head on the pillow, and try to block out the busyness of our lives. Sometimes it is the little voice of doubt that keeps us from sleeping.

Did I make the right decision when I sold the company stock?

I know my husband really wanted to talk today, but I had so much to do!

I missed my daughter's piano recital, but there will be others. The meeting at church was important.

The heart is everything to human life. In our culture, we have neglected this truth and focused on the mind as the center of human life. Ancient Hebrews, like David and Solomon, would have said, "No, the mind is not the center. True life flows from the heart. Everything we do and everything we are—our very destiny—bubbles up from the deep inner spring of the heart."

In its most literal sense, the Hebrew word for *heart* meant the blood-pumping organ in the center of the chest. In its metaphorical usage, however, *heart* became the richest biblical term for the totality of our inner or immaterial nature. This includes such forces as emotion, conscience, thought, and will. The heart is where human life meets the environment. It's the gateway to our feelings, decisions, and relationships. The heart is where we feel the deepest joy and pain.

The Hebrews understood that one of the chief benefits of a pure heart was a clear head, the ability to make good decisions. This is why it is so vital that we exercise great care and vigilantly protect our hearts. And where a pure heart leads and a clear head decides, the eyes, mouth, hands, and feet will follow in safety. "Guard your heart," Solomon says. Then he adds: "Avoid all perverse talk; stay far from corrupt speech. Look straight ahead, and fix your eyes on what lies before you. Mark out a straight path for your feet; then stick to the path and stay safe. Don't get sidetracked; keep your feet from following evil" (Proverbs 4:24-27).

"The Wellspring of Life"

What is a wellspring? The dictionary defines it as a "source of a continual supply."[1] Originally it referred to an inexhaustible supply of life-giving water, such as a well fed by an underground spring. In the frontier, as long as the people were near a wellspring, they had plenty of water. But if the well dried up or if the water source became contaminated, the pioneers were in big trouble.

Something like that happened in 1990, when a lab in North Carolina detected traces of benzene in a bottle of world-famous Perrier water. Benzene is a toxic chemical known to be a carcinogen. The president of Perrier Group of America immediately ordered that all bottles of Perrier be removed from distribution in the U.S. A few days later, Source Perrier in Paris announced a worldwide recall of 160 million bottles of their famous product. It turns out that the water had become tainted when workers had failed to change a filter. The contamination cost the company about $30 million up front, not to mention the financial uncertainty that the public would shy away from Perrier in the future.

In a physical sense, the human heart is a wellspring of life. If the heart stops pumping blood or if the blood is contaminated, it can be fatal. But when Solomon identified the heart as the wellspring of life, he was talking about the core of who we are, not just the blood pump. The inner heart is the artesian source of our identity, personality, thoughts, emotions, and will. If something goes wrong with this wellspring, we are in very serious trouble. No wonder Solomon prefaced his admonition to "guard your heart" with "above all else."

What kinds of contamination are we talking about? From what poison must we guard our hearts? In a word, sin. We live in a culture that is largely hostile to biblical truth, moral purity, and marital fidelity. Our hearts are continuously bombarded by temptations from our human nature, our culture, and the devil himself. At the core, these temptations all seek to draw us away from allegiance to Christ, trust in his Word, and pure devotion to spouse and family.

So, how do you guard your heart? You start by being super cautious about what you allow into your heart and mind. Now, it's virtually impossible to shield yourself from every tempting thought, image, or suggestion. But it's what you do with those temptations that matters. As someone once said, "You can't prevent the birds from flying over your head, but you *can* prevent them from building a nest in your hair." The key to guarding your heart against temptation is to dismiss it—shoo it away—as soon as you recognize it.

You also guard your heart by monitoring your activities. Don't put yourself in places or situations in which you know you are weak to resist temptation. What kinds of books and magazines do you read? What kinds of movies do you watch? What kinds of people do you hang out with? Where do you invest your free time and money? You can avoid many contaminants to the heart by avoiding the settings in which those pollutants are strongest.

If you fail to guard your heart from contamination, everything that flows out of your life will be tainted by the toxins you have allowed to seep into the very source of who you are. A poisoned heart will negatively affect everything you are involved in: your marriage, your parenting, your job, your friendships, and your ministry for the Lord.

Tragically, the contamination of the heart can continue to poison others even after we have departed from this earth. I'm thinking about a young widow named Brenda. On a warm summer evening six weeks after her husband's death, Brenda ventured out to Jim's tool shed to gather some of his things for a yard sale. She found some boxes of his stuff tucked away amongst the oil cans, hedge clippers, and work gloves. Inside these boxes she found snapshots of her husband—scores of them. Yet Jim wasn't alone in these pictures. Other women—a large variety of women—were in the pictures, engaged in sexual acts and lewd poses with Jim. Brenda was devastated by the discovery.

What may have started out for Jim as an adolescent dabbling in pornography had become a hideous adult obsession. His unguarded heart had become contaminated, and his poor widow had to live with the poison. Even after Brenda remarried, the toxic images tainted her memory, clouded her moods, and cast long shadows over her new relationship. Jim may have thought his secret sin wouldn't hurt anyone else, but Brenda and her new husband are still dealing with the fallout from Jim's unguarded heart.

Sin can't be locked in a back closet of the heart. Sooner or later, it will work its way out to the surface, contaminating our lives and the lives of others, especially those dearest to us—our spouses and children. That's the reason for Solomon's somber warning. And that's the reason Barb and I have written this book. Above all else, we need to protect the deep, life-giving wellspring of our hearts because the outflow of our hearts will determine the very story of our lives and the destiny of our marriages and family relationships.

We would like to plant in your imagination a picture from medieval times, a picture that graphically illustrates the importance of guarding our hearts. Barb will share this helpful visual concept with you.

Safe within the Castle Walls

Guarding your heart can be compared to protecting the castles of the Middle Ages, which protected the lives and property of those who lived within their walls. Gary and I are fascinated by these noble structures. Castles first appeared in northwest Europe in the ninth century. Many of the remnants of those early castles are still there. One authority catalogs the remains of at least fifteen hundred castles in England alone.

Do you ever wonder who lived in those cold stone fortresses? Besides the lord and his family, the household of a castle included knights, squires, men-at-arms, a porter who kept the outer door, and watchmen. There were also ministerial and domestic staffs, a steward who administered the estate, and any number of servants. The larger the landholdings, the larger the staff. But one thing was always true: The castle was built to protect those who lived inside it.

The castle's first and foremost line of resistance was its stone wall and towers. The ground in front of the wall was kept free of all cover. If the castle had a moat, the ground was cleared well beyond it. As a result, an approaching enemy would be clearly exposed and defenseless in the open ground. Some large castles kept a year's supply of food on hand. A garrison of sixty men could hold out against an attacking force ten times its number for months on end.

Every castle had its own history of warfare. These family strongholds were typically built on high ground, positioned to command a view of the approaches on all sides. Boiled down to the basics, medieval military science involved the attack and defense of castles. Castles were constructed to defend, and enemies were determined to attack. As the sophistication of the defenses grew, so did the schemes of the attackers.

Castles could be attacked in one of two ways. The most overt was the *frontal attack*. That's where the bad guys rolled right up to the walls and started hammering away with catapults, battering rams, flaming arrows, and hordes of invaders scrambling up long ladders. This head-on approach was an attempt to simply overpower the castle by brute force. However, the strategic placement of the castle along with its massive outer walls gave it an imposing look, and the defenses were usually sufficient to turn back most head-on assaults.

If the frontal attack failed, a second approach might be employed: the *sneak attack*. These sorts of tactics were limited only by the craftiness of an enemy's imagination. If they couldn't knock down the walls, they might attempt to starve the inhabitants out by cutting off their provisions from the outside or, even worse, by damming up or poisoning the castle's water supply. Or attackers might attempt to tunnel under a tower in order to set fire to the supporting timbers.

Another ploy was to take the castle dwellers by surprise with a ruse, something like the famous Trojan horse. Attackers would sometimes dress like peasants to gain entrance and then overpower the unsuspecting inhabitants. Or a devious enemy might propose a fake truce or offer a bribe to a weak-willed inhabitant who would open the castle gate to the enemy.

When a castle was under siege by a powerful or clever invader, it was too late to shore up the defenses. There was no time for replacing rotting timbers in the gate or cementing the walls with fresh mortar. The castle's defenses had to be maintained at all times so that it would be ready for any attack that would come. The lives of those inside depended on it.

THE ENEMIES OF YOUR HEART

Just like the castles of old, your heart and the hearts of your spouse and children are vulnerable to a variety of dangers from without and within. Solomon exhorts us to shore up the castle of our hearts against the enemies of our relationship with Christ, with our spouse, and with our children. This is no time to cut corners, look for shortcuts, or scrimp on essentials. The castle lord who saved a few pieces of silver on low-budget defenses likely paid for his foolishness with his life.

You dare not make the same mistake. Your heart is too valuable. It must be protected at all costs.

A vital prerequisite to shoring up the defense of your heart is to identify the enemies of your heart. The more you know about the nature of the assault, the better prepared you will be to defend against it. Gary and I talk to literally thousands of husbands and wives through our ministry, and we have identified six key areas of attack that are common to most couples. In part 2 of this book, we will devote one chapter to each of the six areas, exploring them in depth. But here is a brief overview of the six critical enemies of your heart:

1. *Job and home pressures.* Many couples allow the pressures of pursuing a career and maintaining a home to push marriage and family relationships to the back burner. When you focus too narrowly on your next promotion or the responsibilities of home management and children's activities, you leave your heart unguarded.

2. *Material distractions.* Most people find the affluence of our culture difficult to resist. The dizzying lust for pleasure, power, money, and position can turn your heart away from the lasting values of nurturing loving relationships.

3. *Relationship pressures.* Everyone around you seems to need something from you—your attention, your support, your energy, your resources. Failing to prioritize your relationships can fragment your heart's devotion.

4. *Sexual temptation.* Both men and women are vulnerable to the temptations of physical and/or emotional infidelity. Failing to establish and maintain relational guardrails can lead to heartbreak in a marriage.

5. *Misguided view of success.* The drive to succeed in this world often prompts healthy competition fueled by pride, envy, and greed. Buy into the world's warped view of success, and you may leave your heart behind.

6. *Passivity and control.* Many marriages are pulled apart from one of two opposite poles: passivity and control. A passive part-

ner abdicates the responsibility of nurturing marriage and family relationships. A controlling partner foists his or her agenda on other family members. Passivity and control in marriage can kill the heart.

Can you feel the battering ram crashing against the gate of your castle? Can you hear the flaming arrows hissing over your head? Can you see the angry army advancing outside the walls? Yes, your heart is under siege—and your spouse's heart is as well! Your marriage hangs in the balance. How can you be sure your defenses will hold up against the multifaceted attack? Is it possible to guard your hearts against the onslaught?

Yes, it is possible—and it is imperative. In part 3 of this book, Gary and I will coach you on a number of vital skills for guarding your heart and your spouse's heart. Equipping your hearts with guarding love is a primary means for divorce-proofing your marriage.

Gary and I are passionate about divorce-proofing America's marriages. Why? Because we have seen the carnage in homes where hearts have been left unguarded. Gary is going to close this chapter by sharing with you a letter he received from a man whose heart is under siege. It is because of this man and his wife—and countless others like them—that we must urge you to guard your heart.

A COUPLE UNDER SIEGE

A few years ago, I received a letter from a man who almost slept through the most crucial battle of his life. By the time he woke up, it was almost too late. Barb and I are grateful that at least he woke up!

I was flying home after speaking at a weekend marriage conference with over a thousand people in attendance. I didn't have a moment to myself until I finally buckled into my airline seat for the first leg of a long flight home. As I prepared for a welcome catnap, I suddenly remembered a letter I had stuffed into my coat pocket during the conference. A man had pressed it into my hand as I was talking with two or three other couples. Finally, in the relative peace of a Chicago-bound flight, I pulled out the letter and read these words:

Hey, Rosberg,

Caught your conference this weekend. You had some pretty powerful stuff to lay on us. I have to admit, I walked in on Friday night pretty arrogant. But that isn't how I left.

I'm thirty-six, married for twelve years. I've been a Christian since high school. What big problems could I have? My wife asked me to go to this conference last year, and I held her off. Too much work on my plate. This year I asked her to go because even I thought our marriage needed a tune-up.

She was a bit hesitant. It wasn't until Saturday night that she filled in the blanks on that one. I thought, Hey, this will be okay. We might even learn a thing or two about communicating on a deeper level. Let me make one thing clear: I love my wife, Gary. I just don't have a good handle on how to lead my home. I've been real busy lately, but she understands.

Or so I thought!

Our marriage has suffered from a lot of what you called erosion. My wife has filled her life with the kids, work, and other stuff. I thought we were rolling along pretty well. Until Saturday night. Now I'm truly scared. I usually go to God for the big-ticket items but try to handle the low-maintenance stuff myself. Well, I blew it. What I thought was low maintenance was anything but. My wife has been hurting. In fact, she may be beyond hurting.

Gary, I thought I was doing okay. Not a great leader of the home, but not bad. In just three days at your conference, I learned what a mess I've made of my life. Now I'm facing the reality of losing my wife and kids! How is it possible that I had my values and priorities so screwed up? The $64,000 question is really this: If I get another shot at this marriage, how am I going to stay in the game and stop myself from reverting to the old habits?

What I'm trying to say, in a roundabout way, is thanks for the wake-up call. For whatever it's worth, you really made me stop and think about how to live my life.

You know what tears me apart, Gary? My wife asked me to go to your conference last year. But I didn't hear her. I had to beg her to go this year, and she didn't want to listen to me. If only I'd had a guy like you last year to look me in the eye and say, "Don't be stupid. Go to the conference." This has been the longest night of my life. Whatever spare prayers you may have, I would greatly appreciate it if you send some out for me.

HOW IS YOUR CASTLE HOLDING UP?

After reading this letter, you may be heading downstairs to check on your spouse. Or you may want to put this book down to give your dear one a call from your office, just to make sure he or she is still there. The wake-up call from this man may have gotten your attention. Barb and I hope so.

Here are three things you can count on.

1. You have a marriage relationship that is worth guarding with your life.

2. Living in a world that is largely hostile to healthy marriages, your hearts will come under attack.
3. You cannot survive these attacks on your own. You and your spouse must stand together against your common foe. You must guard your heart and guard each other's heart. And you need others to stand with you over the long haul—Christians who share your desire for a divorce-proof marriage.

Barb and I want to be counted among your group of supporters. We offer this book and the accompanying workbook to equip your marriage relationship with guarding love. So let's get to work by discussing six perils lying in wait to steal your heart.

Part Two

THE THREATS TO YOUR MARRIAGE

Chapter Three

CAREER AND HOME OUT OF BALANCE

We were all designed by our heavenly Father to work. We're *called* to work. That has been true from the beginning of time. Genesis records, "Then the Lord God planted a garden in Eden, in the east, and there he placed the man he had created. . . . The Lord God placed the man in the Garden of Eden to tend and care for it" (2:8,15).

Work is good. Work is God's idea. The psalmist gives the timeless picture: "People go off to their work; they labor until the evening shadows fall again" (Psalm 104:23).

The division of labor in the average home usually falls into two general categories: work that is done *in* the home—housework, gardening, cooking, cleaning, child care, and the like—and work that is done *outside* the home—gainful employment to support the family. Historically in America, women have been the homemakers, and men have been the wage earners. But in the last several decades the line has blurred between these traditional gender roles. Many wives today are as career-minded as their husbands—or even more so. These couples share the responsibility of earning an income, and they often share the responsibility of housework, cooking, and child care. In some cases, a woman on a career track is the primary wage earner, and her husband—who may or may not have a job of his own—is "Mr. Mom" at home. And with the growing popularity of telecommuting, the various combinations of husband-wife responsibilities seem endless.

When our daughters, Sarah and Missy, were growing up, Barb and I followed the traditional model, and it worked well for us. I went out into the world every day to earn an income while Barb managed the day-to-day duties at home and was onsite for our girls full-time. I was not a stranger to housework and child care; I pitched in where I could and spent time with our daughters. But by reason of our accepted roles, a good deal of my attention and energy was devoted to establishing my counseling career.

As our girls became more independent, Barb felt called to get involved in the ministry with me. And today, as occupants of an empty nest, we are both involved full-time in leading the ministry of America's Family Coaches—a team operation we fully enjoy. We share responsibilities in the office, we share the speaking in our conferences, and we double-team our daily radio program. And when we get home, we work together on whatever needs to be done—cooking, laundry, running the vacuum, or whatever. It's a great partnership.

No matter how you and your spouse divide up responsibilities in your home, you must guard your heart against the twin enemies of allowing your activities outside the home or inside the home to take precedence over your relationship as husband and wife. Yes, building a career and running a home are important, time-consuming, energy-sapping, and—for the most part—fulfilling endeavors. But if you allow your work to rule your heart, your relationship with your spouse and family will suffer dire consequences.

We want to address the two heads of this potential monster separately. First, I want to zero in on the heart danger that comes from an overemphasis on work and career. I am probably talking to most of you husbands and perhaps a number of wives. Later in the chapter, Barb will focus on the perils of an unhealthy preoccupation with responsibilities at home, which will be a temptation to many wives as well as some men.

CAREERS IN CRISIS

Those of you reading this book are involved in a wide range of careers and jobs. You are laborers, executives, sales reps, teachers, customer service agents, public servants, pastors—the list of job titles is almost endless. Some of you work the farm, others work a spreadsheet. Your field may be technical, clerical, legal, medical, agricultural, educational, mechanical, political, or spiritual. Some of you are in your very first job. Others are in your umpteenth.

How do you view your career as a whole and your day-to-day tasks? What drives you to get out of bed, show up at the job site, and put in a good day's work? Is it the money? The prospect of advancement and even more money? The challenge and adventure of your work? The sense of fulfillment at a job well done? The camaraderie with coworkers or clients? Your source of motivation will determine not only how well you work but also the health of your marriage and family life.

LEARNING ABOUT WORK ON THE JOB

I want to tell you about one job I had, a job that required every muscle group in my body and that taxed my mind and emotions to their limits. I trust it will set the stage for a biblical view of any job you become involved in.

In our home state of Iowa, the summer of 1993 will be remembered for the rain that never seemed to end. It began rain-ing here in late spring, and by July 1 the cumulative precipitation had soared far above normal levels. Farmers couldn't work their crops. Parents couldn't send their kids out to play. And each day the soil became more and more saturated.

In the midst of the incessant downpour, I flew off to Atlanta to attend a convention of the Christian Booksellers Association. As soon as I arrived at my hotel room, I clicked on CNN. The lead story immediately transported me back home. There on the screen was my suburb of West Des Moines experiencing serious flooding. News footage showed workers laboring feverishly in the torrential rains, sandbagging the water treatment plant and the river banks. Things had quickly gone from bad to worse since I left home. And meteorologists were predicting even more rain.

I immediately called home to see how Barb and the girls were doing. When the answering machine kicked in, I didn't hear the chipper voices of my two girls as usual. It was Barbara's voice saying wearily, "We can't answer the phone right now. The girls and I are out sandbagging the river. Please call back later."

My shock turned to fear. Here I was in a comfortable Atlanta hotel while my wife and two daughters were sandbagging the river. There was something wrong with that picture. I needed to get home—fast. I grabbed my luggage and headed back to the Atlanta airport.

Barb met me at the airport. I could see the strain in her eyes and face. She had done what had to be done, just like every other able-bodied person in the flood zone. She had helped fight back the river, even injuring her back filling sandbags. She had prayed with our daughters and provided necessary emotional support, assuring them that everything would be all right. It was my turn to take over the helm.

I had been home less than an hour when we got a call from a friend whose shop was about to be engulfed by the river. Before I was off the phone, Barb was into her sandbagging clothes again. I followed her example. The two of us, along with dozens of others, evacuated the shop, an effort accompanied by tears, hugs of support, and incredible teamwork.

On the way home from my first flood job, I received word from my office that the swirling waters had separated one of my clients from his home. He had been directed to a Red Cross shelter in a school gymnasium just six blocks from our home. We joined National Guard troops, Red Cross volunteers, and scores of other people at the shelter to help wherever we were needed. Our first assignment was to fill out forms registering volunteers. Twenty minutes later, I was charged with establishing a counseling program for flood victims in another Red Cross shelter three blocks away.

I will never forget that summer. The experience of serving men, women, and kids during the flood will remain vivid in my memory the rest of my life. I labored with thousands of others, helping to serve meals and hand out clothes. I counseled elderly people fearful of leaving the wreckage of their homes. I helped clean out debris from houses and went back weeks later to help paint those houses.

I can truthfully say it was the best job I ever had. Why? Because I worked as God said we should work: with all my heart. The apostle Paul wrote, "Work hard and cheerfully at whatever you do, as though you were working for the Lord rather than for people. Remember that the Lord will give you an inheritance as your reward, and the Master you are serving is Christ" (Colossians 3:23-24).

ON GOD'S PAYROLL

Whatever you do, God wants you to do it with all your heart. That includes your work, whether it is inside or outside the home. It doesn't matter if you are the governor of your state or the person who cleans the governor's office. You may manage a staff of hundreds or spend all day alone in a tiny cubicle with a computer. It doesn't matter what you do. What matters is *how* you do it. It all comes down to your heart. How do you serve? Willingly? Reluctantly? Selfishly?

When you do a job—any job—you are ultimately working for Jesus Christ. Yes, you receive financial compensation for your labors, but you are actually working for eternal rewards. We are Christ's representative where we work. That's why we need to be wholehearted in whatever we do. Think about the non-Christians you work with. They probably know you are a Christian, and they are watching you work. You claim to be a new creation in Christ. Does the quality of your work and your dedication to the job underscore that positive difference?

Todd, a friend of mine, has a heart for Christ and a desire to reach others for him. He wanted to share his faith with a coworker, but Brett wasn't interested, having had some bad experiences with church as a kid.

At lunch one day, Todd told me about a dilemma he was facing in a work project with Brett. Todd had bid the job, then realized he had significantly underestimated the cost. Should he go back to the customers and face up to possibly losing the contract by informing them of the problem? Or should he manipulate the numbers and squeak by?

Todd knew Brett was watching. Would Todd's faith make a difference? He remembered what the apostle Paul wrote about others watching your work: "This should be your ambition: to live a quiet life, minding your own business and working with your hands, just as we commanded you before. As a result, people who are not Christians will respect the way you live" (1 Thessalonians 4:11-12).

When Todd and I looked at his situation in this biblical context, the conclusion was a no-brainer. Todd made the right call. He went back to the customers and faced the consequences. And Brett wanted to know why he did it.

"You see, Brett," Todd told him, "this faith thing is more than going to church on Sundays. It also affects how I live, how I work."

The Lord tells us to work for him in everything we do. Why? So others can see Christ through us. Jesus is your immediate supervisor. You work to please him. He is also your primary payroll clerk. You work first for his reward. No matter how unpleasant your job may be, your work can be satisfying because you are really serving Jesus Christ.

DANGERS ON THE JOB

Traveling down Interstate 80 recently, I saw flashing lights ahead. Barricades crisscrossed the road, giving ample warning of construction in process. Approaching the site, I saw men and women working hard in the heat of the summer sun while thousands of cars passed by within a few feet. Drivers were warned to slow down and be alert. Nevertheless, some cars whizzed by too fast, endangering the safety of both the workers and other motorists. Some of the lane-marking cones that were meant to steer cars away from equipment and workers had been knocked aside.

All the elements of danger were present in this setting: high rates of speed, workers vulnerable to the elements and to passing motorists, pressures to get the job done on time, excessive traffic.

Sounds like our careers, doesn't it? We move at high speed, trying to accomplish more and more work with less and less time, money, and energy. We are vulnerable to all kinds of elements: office politics, downsizing, sexual temptation, lack of training, excessive competition, deadline pressures. And all this happens in a whirlwind of daily phone calls, appointments, budget crises, personality clashes, conflicting goals—you name it.

Check Your Balance

For most of us, work itself is not inherently dangerous. But any kind of work *out of balance* is dangerous to the health of your marriage and family. What is work out of balance? When your work provides for your family in some areas—such as meeting financial and material needs—but robs your family in other areas—such as emotional, relational, and spiritual health—it is dangerously out of balance.

The apostle Paul wrote strong words about failing to provide for our families: "If anyone does not provide for his relatives, and especially for his immediate family, he has denied the faith and is worse than an unbeliever" (1 Timothy 5:8, NIV). Worse than an unbeliever? Wow! If we do not provide for our families, we are in deep weeds. You must guard your heart against work out of balance.

So what does *provide* mean? Certainly it means tending to physical and material needs. But your spouse and children need more from you than food, shelter, clothing, and an occasional trip to Disney World. They need your understanding, wisdom, and comfort. They need your companionship, time, and attention. They need your spiritual guidance and accountability. You can provide them with the nicest house in town, filet mignon three times a week, and a TV in every room, but if you are not there with them emotionally, relationally, and spiritually, you are not providing for them. That's work out of balance, and it's a sin.

This doesn't mean you don't work hard, apply for promotions, and sometimes put in long hours. It means you save enough of yourself to connect heart-to-heart with your spouse and children. And if you are not connecting as you should, it may mean cutting back on your work or paring down your material needs in order to free up time for the most important people in your life.

Is your work out of balance? You may be working two or three jobs to make ends meet. You may be knocking yourself out to get a bigger house, a newer car, or the latest home theater system. Or maybe work is out of balance for you because it's the only place you feel fulfilled. The stress or tension at home is so thick that you find yourself staying at the office later than ever before, and you sense your family is slipping away from you.

Or perhaps you are in denial. Everyone—from your wife, kids, parents, and friends to the family dog—knows your work schedule is out of balance. You may have been told, but you aren't listening. You have ignored any input because you're afraid to hear the truth. And until a crisis hits, you are likely to continue the pattern.

When you come home so exhausted that you have nothing left for your family, you are in a destructive pattern. When your kids stop talking to you about school, problems, or fun times, you may be out of balance. When you miss family meals three or four times a week and can't remember the last time you attended your child's soccer game or music recital, you have crossed the line.

You can always find another job, but you cannot replace your family. Your heart and your home are under attack. You must guard against work out of balance. Here are three plumb-line questions for guarding your heart:

1. Is your work pleasing to God—your motivation, use of time, attitude toward the job, and the like?
2. Is your family getting choice, generous, and consistent servings of your mental and emotional energy? Do you give them *quantity* time as well as *quality* time?
3. Do you resist being pushed into the danger zone regarding your emotional, mental, and physical health? Are you balancing hard work with plenty of one-on-one time with your spouse and recreation with the whole family?

One evening over dinner, my friend Dennis Rainey challenged me to count the cost of my overburdened schedule at that time. As we were discussing the ministries I was involved in, Dennis put down his fork and said, "Gary, God has given you many arenas of effectiveness for him. You have the potential to enjoy success in any of those areas. But if you aren't careful, you'll spread yourself too thin and become ineffective in your calling as well as in your home. The question you need to ask yourself is not where *can* you succeed but where *must* you succeed."

Wise words from a wise man. The health and growth of our marriages and families demand that we find and maintain balance in our work.

The second major area of work where balance is a key issue is the home. Whether you are a stay-at-home mom or "Mr. Mom," your challenge is to guard your heart and home against work out of balance. Barb will guide us through this section.

TROUBLE ON THE HOME FRONT

Dixie is a thirty-five-year-old wife and stay-at-home mother of four children. With two kids in school and two still in diapers, Dixie's day is wall-to-wall kids. Up before 6:00 A.M., she barely has time for devotions, a cup of coffee, and a five-minute shower before her typical day begins.

- ⊕ 6:20 A.M.—Pick up and snuggle with the early rising fifteen-month-old.
- ⊕ 6:34 A.M.—A few minutes of snuggles with other awaking children coming down the stairs.
- ⊕ 6:44 A.M.—First shift of breakfast for the two toddler boys while the girls get dressed for school.
- ⊕ 6:57 A.M.—Braids or pigtails for the girls while husband Chet showers and dresses for work.
- ⊕ 7:10 A.M.—Second shift of breakfast for everyone else—plus the day's family Bible reading.
- ⊕ 7:29 A.M.—Gather book bags, misplaced homework papers, and lunches for the girls, and hustle them out the door.
- ⊕ 7:41 A.M.—Wave good-bye as Chet takes the girls to school on his way to work.

Dixie plants the boys in front of *Sesame Street* and catches her breath with a second cup of coffee and brief glance at the newspaper. Then it's back to work.

- ⊕ 8:01 A.M.—Clean up the breakfast mess and dress the boys.
- ⊕ 8:26 A.M.—Start the first of three loads of today's laundry.

⊕ 8:35 A.M.—Engage the boys in educational playtime.

⊕ 8:53 A.M.—Work on toilet training with her older son, and change the younger boy's diapers.

⊕ 9:04 A.M.—Work at housecleaning and laundry while breaking up fights and solving minor crises.

⊕ 10:00 A.M.—Put the baby down for a morning nap— three different times.

⊕ 10:16 A.M.—Read books and enjoy one-on-one time with the toddler in between laundry tasks.

⊕ 11:09 A.M.—Load the boys into the minivan for morning kindergarten carpool.

⊕ 11:54 A.M.—Serve the three kids a lunch of macaroni and cheese and apple juice; clean up afterward.

⊕ 12:47 P.M.—Put the boys down for afternoon naps. Pull hamburger from the freezer to thaw for dinner.

⊕ 1:01 P.M.—Enjoy one-on-one time with the kindergartner and help with a homework project.

The rest of Dixie's afternoon—until second grade carpool at 3:40 P.M.—is a collage of pick-up and clean-up tasks, resolving sibling squabbles, changing diapers, folding clothes, and monitoring play activities. Whenever there is a lull, she indulges herself in reading and writing e-mail or playing a computer game. After carpool, the final push begins.

⊕ 4:44 P.M.—Switch on a Veggie Tales video while she sweeps through the house making sure the kids' stuff is put away.

⊕ 5:16 P.M.—Throw together a quick dinner of hamburger gravy over instant mashed potatoes, with steamed broccoli and canned applesauce.

⊕ 5:40 P.M.—Monitor the dinner table alone since Chet works until 6:00 P.M.

⊕ 6:16 P.M.—Ride herd on the children through playtime and homework time.

⊕ 6:43 P.M.—Sit at the table while Chet eats dinner, until one of the kids needs her for something.

⊕ 7:00 P.M.—Begin the nightly two-hour ritual of baths, pajamas, reading time, and bedtime.

By 9:00 P.M. the kids are sleeping and the dinner dishes are done. Dixie and Chet meet in the family room to watch TV and talk about the day. Except Dixie never makes it through their favorite program or finishes the conversation. She dozes on the sofa then slips off to bed before 10:00 P.M.

Dixie's typical day doesn't tell the whole story. Every week there are clarinet lessons, school programs, swimming lessons, weekly women's Bible study at church (the boys go with her), and usually one birthday party for a child's friend or classmate. If you talked to Dixie, she would agree that her life is hectic and that she is overextended. But if she was totally honest with you, she would admit that she wouldn't have it any other way. In fact, Dixie looks for other kid-related activities to keep her schedule at near overload. Pouring herself into the children and the home helps numb the pain of her unfulfilling marriage to Chet. It's easier to stay busy with menus, diapers, lessons, and carpools than to address a dying relationship.

HEARTS AND HOMES LEFT UNGUARDED

Just as there are temptations and opportunities for careers to slip out of balance, women and men whose primary work is the care of home and children can find themselves dangerously unbalanced. Gary and I know this experientially. We have felt the heat of the attack. There is so much to do at home, especially when you factor in the activities and needs of growing children. And it's a twenty-four-hour-a-day job! You are either on duty or on call. You can't punch out at the time clock and leave the job site.

If you allow your daily schedule to be dictated solely by what should be done or could be done around the house, you wouldn't have any time for anything else. Such an unbalanced life leaves any number of important items unguarded and vulnerable to attack. I want to mention a few of them.

Precious relationships are left at risk. Dixie's out-of-control schedule has left her relationship with Chet unguarded. They rarely go out for an evening and never spend a night away from the children. To be sure, they have a number of unresolved conflicts that are painful to address. But by retreating into her home and children, Dixie is leaving her most precious relationship unguarded. The couple will never resolve their issues and recapture their marriage dream until Dixie crawls out of the "bomb shelter" of her home responsibilities and gives Chet her heart.

All relationships need daily maintenance, an occasional tuneup, and time for enjoyment. When your busyness at home—no matter how necessary or well-meaning—stifles your most precious relationships, your home life is out of balance.

Spiritual oneness and fellowship come under attack. Nick couldn't pass up the lucrative buyout and early retirement offered by his company. So at age fifty-seven, he stays home while his wife, Maria, still works at a job she loves. Nick's days are busier than when he had a job. Along with housework, gardening, and cooking chores, he volunteers at their large church, where he has been a respected deacon for twenty-six years. He spends most afternoons visiting and praying with shut-ins. He is so busy ministering to the spiritual needs of others that he doesn't minister to Maria spiritually. He always said they would start praying and reading the Bible together when he had more time. But Nick and Maria have never prayed together in their thirty-six-year marriage.

Many important elements go into keeping a home and family running smoothly. Few are more important than nurturing the spiritual lives of your spouse and children. If you "just can't find the time" to pray and read the Bible with your family members, your balance is dangerously off.

Unity and interdependence are threatened. Winnie's husband, Frank, runs a small company, and he is on the road three to five days each week. Winnie likes to think she runs a company at home. She is efficient and resourceful at keeping herself and the kids on task when Frank is gone. In fact, she prides herself in running such a tight ship, and she loves making the decisions. When Frank is home, Winnie considers him underfoot, a fifth wheel in her smooth-running operation. She enjoys her independence so much that she sometimes wishes Frank would travel more.

You can become so absorbed in your own "kingdom" at home that you need your partner less and less. When unity and interdependence in a family relationship are replaced by a mentality of fierce independence, your marriage and family have drifted off center.

Emotions and morals come under attack. Curtis hates to admit that his wife, Margo, is the career person in the family, but it's true. Margo has been with her company for nineteen years and is only a year or two away from a vice president's position. But Curtis hasn't held a steady job for nearly two years. So while he waits for his ship to come in, he takes care of the house and does the cooking. Except for a job interview or two each week,

Curtis is home alone in their suburban tract. He has become something of a neighborhood hero to several women whose husbands are rarely home during daytime hours. One woman has been especially friendly, igniting desires that his working wife seldom ignites. Curtis begins looking for reasons to stop by his neighbor's house.

Temptations to emotional and moral compromise can be found at home just as much as they can be on the job. If you invest inappropriate amounts of emotional energy in relationships with people other than your spouse, you are treading on thin moral ice.

SACRIFICING TO GUARD YOUR HOME

What would you give to keep yourself, your spouse, and your home from being trapped in a scenario like any of these? Would you be willing to give up some of your time? Would you postpone or cancel some projects around the house? Would you agree to reduce your family income? It may take drastic measures to get your home back in balance. But it is worth the sacrifice to guard the hearts and relationships of the dearest people in your life.

Gary and I made a drastic move in order to guard our home from the dangers of being out of balance. When our first daughter was born, Gary was earning $7,200 a year as a probation officer, and I was making about the same as a teacher. Back then the dollar went a lot farther, but it was still a tight squeeze for us to make ends meet.

It had been our plan for me to stay home when we had children. But once Sarah arrived, our plan seemed unrealistic. How could we survive on Gary's small salary alone, especially with the increased cost of caring for a newborn? But we decided to do it anyway. We wanted our kids to grow up with a parent at home. So I quit my teaching job and became a stay-at-home mom.

It was tough. We scrimped and cut back and sometimes did without. It was a sacrifice, but we made it willingly because our family was more important to us than whatever a second salary could buy. Soon after we made the decision, God blessed Gary with a promotion and a raise to almost $10,000. We were still bringing home less than our combined income would have been, but God continued to provide. And I spent the majority of my time at home as our two girls grew up.

There were other sacrifices. Gary was the full-time wage earner, but when he invested some of his free time trying to lighten my load at home and when he asked what he could do to help me, it sounded like music to my ears. His attitude and his sacrifice pulled me through some long, hard days at home.

I'm happy to report that Sarah, who is now a mother herself, and her husband, Scott, have made the same decision. Sarah was involved with us in the ministry, and it was a great job. But they decided that Sarah would quit her job to be at home with our grandson, Mason. It has been a sacrifice for them just as it was for us. But we can see the rewards already. Mason is bonding with his mom and dad and growing in every way. And we know that Jehovah Jireh, the God who provides, will honor their commitment and meet their needs just as he did for Gary and me.

We don't know what it might cost you to guard your hearts and home from a dangerous work imbalance. But no matter how much time, energy, and resources you expend to keep your career and home in balance, the dividends you reap from your guarding love will make it all worthwhile.

As you review your world of work, whether it be in the home, in the marketplace, or both, how are you doing at balancing your roles? Where do you need to step back and ask some hard questions about how you may be sacrificing your family at the altar of success? What changes can you make to help guard your family? We want to challenge you with the same challenge Dennis Rainey brought to Gary. The issue is not where you *can* succeed but where you *must* succeed. Success is fleeting, but relationships are eternal. Let's invest in the eternal together!

Chapter Four

THE ALLURE OF STATUS AND STUFF

THE FOLLOWING STORY IS SADLY REPRESENTATIVE OF MANY couples who have paid a dear price for leaving their hearts and homes unguarded.

Raul and Sonya had great jobs, a beautiful home, and a handsome teenage son, Jason. Raul was vice president of a financial software firm, raking in a low six-figure income, and Sonya was a bank manager. They had a loaded new Suburban, a smaller SUV, a little sports car, and a ski boat. Raul belonged to a prestigious golf club in town and was a big sports fan. Sonya owned several horses and spent lots of time riding and showing them. The couple worked hard and enjoyed all the perks and toys their titles and income afforded them.

But high-powered careers and expensive amusements also worked against this couple and their family. Raul traveled three weeks out of the month, and on the weekends the husband and wife often went their separate ways. Raul played golf with the guys, and Sonya went riding with her friends. And when they were at home together, if there was any kind of sporting event on TV, Raul was planted in front of it. Since it wasn't much fun to be home with Raul when he was glued to a game, Sonya often retreated to the stable to groom her horses.

When Jason got involved in the youth ministry of a nearby church, Raul and Sonya were pleased. And when the youth pastor invited Jason's parents to bring their fancy boat to the lake for an afternoon of skiing with the youth group, they gladly agreed. Jason had already become a Christian, and soon Raul and Sonya gave their lives to Christ and began attending church with their son.

Both Raul and Sonya began to grow spiritually. But fitting a new Christian faith into their busy lives of work and pleasure proved to be a challenge. Their hobbies often kept them from church. They also became preoccupied with buying and renovating a large home with sufficient property for Sonya's horses. Then Raul got the itch for a fancier sports car. All the while, Raul's sports fanaticism and Sonya's obsession with her horses kept them virtual strangers in their own home.

Then the sky fell in on their marriage. Quite by accident, Sonya overheard a conversation between Raul and his secretary. It was clear that they had been carrying on an affair for some time. When Sonya confronted Raul about it, he confessed. The couple is still together, but it has been a rocky road of reconciliation, and Sonya still considers divorce an option. In the meantime, they continue to work and play as hard as ever.

Even though Raul and Sonya's toys and time commitments may be different from yours, their story alerts us to another grave danger to the health of marriage and family. We are perpetually distracted from our devotion at home by a collection of things Barb and I have identified under the heading "status and stuff." If you intend to divorce-proof your family, you need to recognize and guard against any amusements and involvements—as harmless as they may be in themselves—that will diminish your devotion to your spouse and children.

BLINDED BY DISTRACTIONS

In our most noble moments of aspiration and vision, we set lofty goals for growing in Christ and bonding with our spouse and children. But those moments of idealism are followed by weeks and months of the daily grind and weekly duties. Our wonderful goals and best intentions soon appear dull and commonplace next to the sparkling, alluring distractions coming at us from all sides.

What are the distractions in your life? Could they be any of the following?

Pleasure. Do you live for the weekend, good times, parties and fun, rest and relaxation? Would you rather be watching TV, playing golf, or attending a concert than anything else? Are your pleasure pursuits a bone of contention in your relationships at home?

Power. Are you captivated by the next rung on the corporate ladder? Do you find yourself striving for authority or control in your relationships and the organizations you belong to? Are you unhappy when you don't receive the recognition you deserve in committees, commissions, or task forces?

Possessions. Are you under the illusion that getting the next raise, making that big sale, or winning the lottery will make your problems go away? Are you discontent with what you have, always yearning for a bigger home, newer car, nicer wardrobe, or the latest grown-up toys?

Position. Is it vitally important to you to be known as chairperson, vice president, president, office manager, team leader, or some other title? Would you move to another area of responsibility if you were offered a more prestigious position?

Now, there is nothing intrinsically wrong with any of these four pursuits. Each of us experiences in varying degrees the distractions of pleasure, power, possessions, and position in life. But Barb and I are convinced that any of these elements can distract you from the more important endeavors of loving and nurturing your family relationships. These distractions don't deliver what they promise. They are not worthy substitutes for rich and loving relationships at home. And if you won't take our word for it, consider the advice of someone who experienced more pleasure, power, possessions, and position than you or your spouse will ever know.

THE MAN WHO HAD IT ALL

Like everyone today, King Solomon searched for deep satisfaction and fulfillment in life. But unlike the rest of us, Solomon had virtually everything at his fingertips. Nothing was beyond his grasp. Consider his testimony:

> I said to myself, "Come now, let's give pleasure a try. Let's look for the 'good things' in life." But I found that this, too, was meaningless. "It is silly to be laughing all the time," I said. "What good does it do to seek only pleasure?" After much thought, I decided to cheer myself with wine. While still seeking wisdom, I clutched at foolishness. In this way, I hoped to experience the only happiness most people find during their brief life in this world.
>
> I also tried to find meaning by building huge homes for myself and by planting beautiful vineyards. I made gardens and parks, filling them with all kinds of fruit trees. I built reservoirs to collect the water to irrigate my many flourishing groves. I bought slaves, both men and women, and others were born into my household. I

also owned great herds and flocks, more than any of the
kings who lived in Jerusalem before me. I collected
great sums of silver and gold, the treasure of many kings
and provinces. I hired wonderful singers, both men and
women, and had many beautiful concubines. I had
everything a man could desire!

So I became greater than any of the kings who ruled
in Jerusalem before me. And with it all, I remained
clear-eyed so that I could evaluate all these things.
(Ecclesiates 2:1-9)

Pleasure. Power. Possessions. Position. Solomon had it all.
In his drive to please his aching soul, he lived over the edge. He
sought out all the pleasures he could find. The king continues:
"Anything I wanted, I took. I did not restrain myself from any
joy. I even found great pleasure in hard work, an additional reward for all my labors" (v. 10). And his conclusion? "But as I
looked at everything I had worked so hard to accomplish, it was
all so meaningless. It was like chasing the wind. There was nothing really worthwhile anywhere" (v. 11).

He doesn't say, "I didn't gain much." He doesn't say, "I could
have gained more if I struck a balance." Solomon concludes that
nothing was gained! Can you hear the pain in his words? He is a
broken man.

But he isn't finished with his evaluation. He has learned to
see distractions even in the pursuit of human wisdom: "Then I
turned my thoughts to consider wisdom, and also madness and
folly. What more can the king's successor do than what has already been done? I saw that wisdom is better than folly, just as
light is better than darkness. The wise man has eyes in his head,
while the fool walks in the darkness; but I came to realize that
the same fate overtakes them both. Then I thought in my heart,

'The fate of the fool will overtake me also. What then do I gain by being wise?' I said in my heart, 'This too is meaningless' " (vv. 12-15, NIV).

Notice where Solomon did his deep thinking: in his *heart,* not in his *head.* Solomon knew that his heart was the wellspring of his life. After listing the pain of his varied pursuits of satisfaction and the worthlessness of his many accomplishments, he comes to the heartfelt conclusion that chasing after these distractions leads to zero profitability in life.

Take a clue from the wisest man who ever lived. The unwholesome pursuit of pleasure, power, possessions, and position will net you nothing of significant and eternal consequence. Instead, as Raul and Sonya have discovered, running after these distractions will work against your dreams for your marriage and family. Guard your heart and your home against these distractions at all costs.

Let's take a closer look at pleasure, power, possessions, and position to better identify the inherent dangers in each.

The Pain in Pleasure

How would you complete the following statement? After a grueling week of work at home or on the job, there's nothing better than . . .

- ⊕ Kicking off my shoes and parking myself in front of the TV.
- ⊕ Shopping until I drop.
- ⊕ Heading for the golf course, tennis court, bowling alley, fishing hole, or ballpark.
- ⊕ Snuggling up with a good book or stack of magazines.
- ⊕ Taking in a movie or two at the local multiplex.

- ⊕ Losing myself in a hobby (scrapbooking, woodworking, coin collecting, rubber stamping, etc.).
- ⊕ Digging up the flower beds and trimming the hedges.

We love life's occasional pleasures. They are a welcome diversion from the day-to-day grind, and there's nothing wrong with them—as long as we keep them in balance. It's when the pursuit of pleasure spills over the boundaries that it becomes a danger to our commitment to God, to our spouse and children, and to our own physical and emotional well-being.

Solomon failed to keep his pleasures in balance, and they eventually destroyed his nation. How about you? Are your pleasures out of balance? When it comes to your discretionary time and money, which comes first: your pleasures or your family? Is your motto "Work hard, play hard, family hardly at all"?

Perhaps you need a second opinion when answering these questions. Ask your spouse and children if they feel they are playing second fiddle to your pleasures. And ask God too. Have you tried looking at your pleasures from his point of view? Solomon's father, King David, had something to say about pleasure:

- ⊕ "You will show me the way of life, granting me the joy of your presence and the pleasures of living with you forever." (Psalm 16:11)
- ⊕ "Take delight in the Lord, and he will give you your heart's desires." (Psalm 37:4)
- ⊕ "[The Lord] fills my life with good things." (Psalm 103:5)

Your Father in heaven wants you to find pleasure even more than you do. And he is at the heart of genuine pleasures that truly satisfy. Guard your heart and your home against cheap imitations and harmful excesses.

POWER PLAY

Most of us men, as well as a surprising number of women, have been jockeying for power since we were little kids, pushing and shoving our way to be first, get the most, and have the best. The desire for excessive power springs up from the selfishness of our old nature. Grabbing after power is one way we indulge that selfishness.

As with other distractions, power in itself is not a bad thing as long as it is used constructively. Taking control of a situation is not wrong unless you run roughshod over others to get what you want. Telling people what to do can be helpful and productive unless you usurp someone else's authority or act like a tyrant. Striving to be first is healthy unless you sabotage your competition or exert unfair or dishonest advantage.

So how can we approach power in a healthy way? The answer is to submit your appetite for power to God. You must allow God to be the only source of your power and the governor over its expression in your life. Again, King David has some good advice in the Psalms:

- ⊕ "God arms me with strength." (18:32)
- ⊕ "The Lord protects me from danger—so why should I tremble?" (27:1)
- ⊕ "The God of Israel gives power and strength to his people." (68:35)

One sure way to guard your heart against an unhealthy "power surge" is to look to God as the source of your power. He will guide you to the right kind of power to be used in the right way at the right time for the right purposes. If you submit your quest for power to him, you won't get distracted by seeking power or using it wrongly.

POSSESSED BY POSSESSIONS

Remember the line in the old Beatles' song, "Can't Buy Me Love"? Solomon wrote something very similar a few millennia earlier: "I collected great sums of silver and gold, the treasure of many kings and provinces. . . . It was all so meaningless" (Ecclesiastes 2:8, 11). Solomon purchased and possessed to an extreme and was no closer to contentment with all he acquired.

According to 1 Kings 3:13, God is the One who made Solomon wealthy, just as he promised to do. So we know that an abundance of money and possessions is not the real problem. What matters is your heart attitude toward getting, having, and using the things you have. In other words, do you possess your possessions, or do they possess you?

How much stuff is enough? Our perpetual answer seems to be, "When I have just a little more, I'll have enough." Perhaps a better question to ask is, "How am I accumulating what I have and why am I doing it?" Barb and I are all for setting financial goals and trying to achieve them. But we won't do it at the cost of our relationships with God, with family, or with others. And we will not step outside higher goals relating to what God has called us to and equipped and gifted us for. Don't allow money or possessions to blur your vision of what God is doing in your life.

God has as much to say in his Word about money and wealth, about buying and possessing, as about almost any other subject. We have plenty of guidelines in the Scriptures for doing what's right when it comes to money. Perhaps the best guideline to start with is what Jesus said in Luke 16:13: "You cannot serve both God and money." Money can be a very helpful servant, but it is the worst possible master.

Barb and I know people who are possessed by money and possessions. They have some dollar figure stuck in their heads—so many hundreds of thousands or millions of dollars. Or they have an itemized list of the treasures they plan to accumulate. And these people have decided that life is hollow and meaningless until they achieve that golden plateau of affluence. So, they work like dogs, distracted by the accumulation of stuff, and completely miss out on real life.

You don't need a specific dollar amount or detailed wish list in mind to be consumed by the pursuit of possessions. And you don't need to be accumulating stuff in order for it to possess you. It's in the heart that lust and covetousness do their real damage. As someone has said, we in our debt-ridden society are addicted to spending money we don't have on things we don't need to keep up with people we don't know.

The generation before mine endured the Great Depression, earned every penny of their money, saved wisely, and lived frugally. But nearly everyone in our generation has grown up in the "good life" and has never done without. How will we handle the wealth that is being passed on to us? Probably the same way we handle it in our own homes today. Many people spend every dollar they earn—plus some—mortgaging themselves to the hilt, maxing out their credit cards, and living on the brink of financial disaster. Very few are good stewards of their money and possessions.

Whether you like it or not, we all live in a world where a certain amount of money and possessions is essential. And the more you have, the more comfortably you can live. So earn what you can, spend it well, and be good stewards of whatever you have. But guard your heart against the distraction of wanting, getting, and having more, more, more.

ELEVATED POSITION

Let's be honest: Having a respected title, accepting a key responsibility, or being recognized for your achievements makes you feel real good. Climbing to the next rung on the corporate ladder, being chosen to lead an influential committee, or having your name and title on the office door cries out, "You are really important!"

But your best effort to seek and strive for these positions is, to quote Solomon, like "chasing the wind" (Ecclesiastes 2:11). Eventually, the lofty position you worked so hard to achieve will belong to someone else. You may be the best chairperson, manager, supervisor, or whatever, but there is probably someone younger and better educated just waiting for you to slip up. If you died tonight, a perfectly adequate replacement would likely be in your chair by noon tomorrow.

Furthermore, if positions are so important to you, you won't be satisfied for long where you are. You will crave the next rung, more responsibility, a bigger office, or a more important assignment. Positions come and go. If you are distracted by the thirst for position or prominence, you will be frustrated and unfulfilled wherever you are. And it may only rob vital attention and devotion from your spouse and children.

It's not wrong to improve your position of authority and influence, whatever it might be. But there is also something to be said for blooming where you are planted and being the best at what you do now, especially if it allows you greater opportunity for service and ministry to your family.

Before I wrap up this chapter, Barb is going to address another area in which we must be on our guard.

BEWARE WHEN YOU COMPARE

Gary and I have noticed a more subtle home-disrupting distraction than those described above. It's not as obvious as clamoring and jostling for pleasure, power, possessions, or position. In fact, you might not even be aware of the trait—especially in yourself. Perhaps because I am a woman, I see it more clearly in women. But I have also noticed how both men and women have negatively influenced their spouses with this sinister distraction.

It's the comparison trap. Here the emphasis is not so much on what you have, what you do, or how much influence you wield. Rather, it's on how favorably your status and stuff compares with that of others. You may feel driven to make sure you measure up to—or exceed—the standards of the people you want to impress. Those who compare don't need the best of everything; they just need something a little better than those around them.

You can be distracted by comparisons on many different levels. For example, you may be tempted to compare yourself with others in one or more of these areas:

- The square footage of your house
- The achievements of your children
- The horsepower of your boat engine or the amperage of your home theater
- Your Sunday morning wardrobe
- The value of your antiques
- The size of your DVD or CD collection

- ⊕ The brand names of your clothing, furniture, or appliances
- ⊕ The productivity of your vegetable garden
- ⊕ Your golf handicap

The pitfall of comparing is the sense of dissatisfaction it sparks. Whenever you are "one-upped" by someone in a category you value, instead of rejoicing with them in their good fortune, you feel bad for yourself. You begin to look for ways you can get what he or she has—or something even better. Or you may vent your dissatisfaction on your spouse. For example, a wife may communicate to her husband, "If you earned a better salary, maybe I could have a china cabinet like hers." Or a husband may complain, "If you weren't so tight with the budget, I could buy a faster computer like the guys in the office have."

Don't put that kind of pressure on yourself or your spouse. It's no crime to wish and plan for nicer things and better conditions. But instead of living in dissatisfaction and disappointment, learn to say with the apostle Paul, "I have learned how to get along happily whether I have much or little. I know how to live on almost nothing or with everything. I have learned the secret of living in every situation, whether it is with a full stomach or empty, with plenty or little" (Philippians 4:11-12).

Gary is going to close this chapter with a personal example of the kind of damage distractions can wreak on a family relationship.

DAMAGE CONTROL

Barb is referring to an incident that happened over a dozen years ago, when I was writing my first book. I spent most of my time writing in my basement study. Because I had a full-time counseling practice, I wrote on weekends and in the early mornings. Since it was my first literary "baby," I was really into it—to the point of distraction. On some weekday mornings when our girls would come downstairs on their way to school to say good-bye, I would be so engrossed in writing that I wouldn't connect with them and give them the attention they needed, something I should have delighted in.

When I finished the book, Barb told me that Missy, who was about eight at the time, had really suffered from my being so absorbed in writing. She didn't feel as connected to me as she once had. I felt terrible, and I decided to do something about it.

Soon afterward I was invited to speak at a conference in Orlando. I agreed to accept, with one stipulation: that Missy would come with me. The organization agreed, and Missy and I boarded the plane with a little wall between us.

At the conclusion of the conference, Missy and I headed off for a few days enjoying the Magic Kingdom and the Florida beaches. During one of my braver moments I asked a difficult question: "Missy, how much damage did I do to our relationship by writing this book?"

"Dad," she said, "I don't want to get sad-spirited tonight."

Ouch! A direct hit from one of the most precious people in my life! "I know, honey," I said, "but sometimes we need to be sad-spirited if it leads to sharing our hearts."

So she opened up. "The hardest thing, Dad, was when I came downstairs before school to tell you something and you would say, 'Just a minute, honey, let me finish this thought on the computer.' Sometimes I waited and waited, but you never looked up. So I just went off to school."

We talked about it, and I apologized and asked for Missy's forgiveness, which she granted. The wall between us was removed. We laughed, we played, we stayed up late, we ate ice cream, we rode rides, we strolled the beach hand in hand picking up seashells. When we walked off the plane on a cold, Iowa winter day, Barb said she could see the sparkle back in Missy's eyes. I only wish I had not robbed my daughter of those months of connection with me.

Distractions. They get in the way, and before you know it, time has slipped through your fingers. You turn around, and your kids are grown and gone. The questions race through your mind: How did they grow up so fast? Where has the time gone? What have I missed with my kids? How could I have been so preoccupied with other things?

Distractions. You are absorbed in them, and they seem so important. Meanwhile, your spouse's needs are not being met. He or she begins seeking intimacy and fulfillment in other things and relationships.

Solomon failed to guard his heart against distractions, and it cost him his heart, his nation, and his family. He lost the relational and spiritual connection with his son Rehoboam and never got it back. Rehoboam's sad epitaph in Scripture reads, "He was an evil king, for he did not seek the Lord with all his heart" (2 Chronicles 12:14).

So, guard your heart and home against distractions that can rob you of your connection with God, your spouse, and your children. No achievement, experience, or treasure justifies such a loss. Where do you need to pull back from some of your own distractions right now and reconnect to those who call you their husband, dad, mom, or wife? How would your family say you are distracted? What is one thing you can do *today* to lead you back to strengthening your marriage and family?

Chapter Five

PEOPLE PRESSURE

LIBBY'S FRANTIC LIFE LEAVES HER DIZZY. SHE FEELS LIKE A juggler trying to keep several plates spinning at the same time. She tries to improve her relationship with her husband, Arch, but he can't seem to get past his anger and frustration from their last blowup. The conflict has Libby stressed to the max, and she doesn't know how to repair the hurts they both feel. What was once a warm and enjoyable marriage has turned cool and distant.

Meanwhile, Libby's relationship with her two teenagers is nothing like it used to be. They are out of control, and they don't respect her authority when she tries to draw the line. She urges Arch to support her in disciplining them, but he isn't much help. She would like to be friends with her kids again, but they don't seem interested.

At the same time, Libby's aging parents are increasingly needy and dependent. They call her every day, asking for something—a ride to the doctor's office, help with this and that—or just to talk. Her mom and dad were always so independent and self-reliant, so their rapid decline has been downright scary. Libby's older sister is another concern. Since Maggie's divorce, she has leaned on Libby for comfort and encouragement.

Arch also has a number of relational plates spinning in his life. In addition to the concerns at home with Libby and the kids,

Arch is embroiled in office politics at the government agency where he works. A longtime friend and onetime subordinate was kicked upstairs ahead of him, and Arch isn't sure their friendship will survive. Arch and his boss don't see eye to eye on many issues. And the divorcée in Accounting has been subtly hitting on him. Arch struggles to maintain a Christian attitude and testimony in this hotbed of interaction.

As chairman of the Building Committee at church, Arch has to deal with a wide range of attitudes and perspectives. Getting committee members to head in the same direction is like driving a team of wild horses. He has to referee squabbles, correct mistakes, and push each member to complete his or her tasks. And the pastor is breathing down his neck every week to get plans approved for the educational wing.

Libby and Arch don't think they can keep their wobbly relational plates aloft for much longer. And they are secretly afraid that the first relationship to fall may be their own.

You Can't Please All of the People All of the Time

If you are anything like Libby and Arch, you live in a relational pressure cooker much of the time. And Barb and I are right in there with you. Doesn't it seem that people all around us need something from us or want something from us? We're not saying that these involvements are necessarily bad; they just tend to keep us very busy—sometimes too busy. And when we are too busy with too many people pressures, some of the most important ones may go unattended.

How many relational plates are you trying to maintain? How many of the following relationships are you involved in right now?

- Your spouse
- Your children—including stepchildren and your children's spouses
- Your grandchildren
- Your parents—including birth parents, stepparents, godparents
- Your spouse's parents
- Your siblings and their families
- Your grandparents
- Other extended family members—uncles, aunts, cousins, etc.
- Your circle of friends
- Your nearest neighbors
- Your superiors, peers, subordinates, and clients at work
- Committees, classes, and groups at church
- Civic organizations, service clubs, and hobby groups

At some time or another, most of the people in your relational circle will come to you for something—your time, your help, your money, your attention, your prayers, your advice. Some of them will come occasionally, others will come often, and a few will be on your doorstep frequently—and sometimes at the most inopportune times. On some days it seems they all want a piece of you at the same time.

Take a typical evening, for example. Your wife wants you to fix the leak in the shower, and she's a little upset that you didn't do it last weekend. Your daughter needs help with her geometry. The assistant pastor calls and wants you to visit a couple of shut-ins with him tonight. A friend wants to come over and watch the game on your big-screen TV. Your mother has been bugging you to come see her. Your son begs you to take him to the mall to buy a video game. And you have barely finished your dinner! These are all reasonable demands. How do you keep these relationships from crashing to the floor?

And since your relationships at every level consist of imperfect people—including you—there will be conflicts and pressures as well as legitimate needs and wants. People will make unfair demands of you, take advantage of you, gossip about you, lie to you, waste your time, borrow things and not return them, try to lay a guilt trip on you, and the like. Conflict and betrayal in any relationship is painful, but it really hurts when it comes from those you love the dearest or need the most.

Relational pressures are always a threat to marriage and family, even when they do not originate in the family. What do you do when these pressures hit? How do you resolve the inevitable relational conflicts, especially when you're struggling through several at the same time? How do you resolve these conflicts while maintaining other important relationships? And how do you guard your heart and home from the damage of relational pressures?

Barb is going to help you apply guarding love to your many relationships. She will coach you through three basic principles for standing guard against the harmful cross fire of relational pressure and conflict.

SURVIVING PEOPLE PRESSURE

Gary and I believe you can handle your many relational pressures, including those between you and your spouse, without seeing all your plates crash to the floor. It takes planning and resolve, but it can be done. Here are three steps to get you started.

Keep First Things First
You may have already concluded that you can't keep many relationships spinning at the same speed for long, especially when

some of them are in conflict. If you haven't reached this conclusion, you need to. We all have a limited amount of time, energy, and capacity for people. So the first step to guarding your heart against a big crash is to prioritize your relationships. Here is the order we suggest.

1. *Take care of your own basic needs.* At first glance, this may seem a little self-centered and self-serving. After all, as Christians we are taught, "Don't be selfish. . . . Be humble, thinking of others as better than yourself" (Philippians 2:3). And yet if we continue to give and give and give to others without refilling our own tanks, we will have nothing to give. This reminds me of the announcement about oxygen masks we hear on the airplane before each flight: "Please place the oxygen mask on your face before assisting your child with his mask." The message behind the announcement is clear: You cannot help your child if you pass out from lack of oxygen. The same principle applies in our relationships. You can't give something you don't have.

Perhaps that's why Jesus instructed us to "Love your neighbor as yourself" (Matthew 22:39). He didn't command us to love our neighbor *better than* ourselves, but *as* we love ourselves. He assumes that we already have a healthy self-love that helps us love others and meet their needs.

For some reason, men in general seem to be better at meeting their own needs than women are. I meet many, many women who are running on empty, and their marriages are suffering because of it. Wives and mothers are often so busy meeting the needs of their families that they fail to refill their own tanks. And going through life with low physical, emotional, and spiritual reserves leaves them vulnerable to many threats that can disconnect them from their husbands and children. The bitterness that often surfaces can result in anger, which can lead to inappropriate emotional—and sometimes physical—attachments.

What kind of self needs are we talking about? The basics are the same for women and men. First, meet your own spiritual needs by spending time with God in prayer and in his Word. Second, meet your own physical needs by eating sensibly and exercising regularly. Third, meet your own emotional needs by saving a little time in your day for yourself. This may include a few minutes for reading, working on a hobby, visiting with a friend, whatever. Attending to this first priority will equip you for meeting your other relational challenges.

2. *Zero in on your spouse.* Your relationship with your spouse should come right after your relationship with God. You need your trusted friend and soul mate in the midst of stressful times. You don't have to struggle through your other relational pressures alone. In fact, God doesn't intend for you to do it alone. He announced shortly after creating Adam, "It is not good for the man to be alone. I will make a companion who will help him" (Genesis 2:18). So guarding your spouse's heart and the health and intimacy of your marriage is your next highest priority.

In part 3 of this book, we will coach you in many skills for nurturing your relationship with your spouse and guarding your hearts and home. At this point let me equip you with one vital question to ask one another, not only in the heat of people pressures but also when things are going well. This question, and your response to the answers you receive, will communicate to your spouse that he or she is number one among your human relationships.

The question is this: "What do you need from me today?" You can show your concern, care, and consideration for your spouse by tuning in to his or her needs in this way. You may know your spouse well enough to take some accurate guesses about what he or she needs from you. For example, if your spouse comes home from a very stressful day at work, you know he or she would welcome a fifteen-minute back rub. Or if the kids were acting like little bandits all day, you know your spouse needs you to take over while he or she gets out of the house for an hour. But how much better when you eliminate the guess-work and say, "Honey, I'm here for you today. What can I do to help you?"

You can be more specific with your offer of loving assistance. Here are a few examples:

⊕ "You're having a good day. Is there anything I can do to make it better?"

⊕ "I know it is difficult for you caring for your parents. I want to help. Tell me what I can do."

⊕ "What do you need from me as we deal with our son's rebellious behavior?"

⊕ "I'm sure you were hurt when your friend betrayed you. What can I do to help you right now?"

⊕ "You are struggling at work, and you feel as if it is eating you alive. I want to be with you in your struggle. What do you need me to do?"

⊕ "I know the stress from your sister's marriage problems is piling up on you. What do you need most from me right now—a hug, a prayer, some space, a quiet walk together?"

In order for this skill to work, of course, each of you must be ready to verbalize your needs to one another, even when your partner does not ask the key question. For example, sometimes I say to Gary, "I need you to sit with me and hold me" or "Please let me talk through the details." Or he may say to me, "I need you to let me express what I'm thinking" or "Cut to the bottom line so I know where this is going."

Typically, women are a little better at verbalizing the emotional side of our needs, and men seem more skilled at expressing the cognitive side. So when you talk about needs with your spouse, make sure you spend some time on his or her "side" of the issue. Men, ask how your wife feels in an area of need. Women, ask what your husband is thinking about an area of need.

As you keep each other first and strive to meet needs, you will help guard against the negative impact of other people pressures in your life.

Maintain Peripheral Vision

As you focus together on your most important relationship, you can still note and monitor the needs in other relationships around you. This is where peripheral vision comes in.

For example, let's say your wife calls you in the middle of an important meeting at work to tell you that her father has just been hospitalized and things look pretty serious. You kick into automatic pilot, assuring her that you are on your way, providing a thirty-second explanation to your coworkers, and then racing out the door. On the twenty-minute drive to meet your wife at the hospital, your mind floods with dark what-if questions: "What if he doesn't pull through? What if my wife needs something from me I don't know how to provide? What if our kids get frightened for their grandfather?"

As you pull into the parking lot, you see your five-year-old son looking through the window of the waiting room. He looks big-eyed and pale—needing his dad. Hurrying inside, you jump in with both feet to meet needs. You embrace your wife, who can finally let the tears flow. Your little boy hangs on to your leg for dear life. You wrap a reassuring arm around his shoulders and assure him that you will stay with him. As other family members arrive, you also comfort them, answer their questions, and still keep a keen eye on your wife—her needs come first.

Or imagine that your husband, a church elder, must confront another elder for inappropriate sexual behavior. Your spouse is personally devastated over his friend's moral failure. When you ask what he needs from you, he asks you to drive with him to the elders' meeting and wait outside for him. You agree, then take his hands and pray with him for God's compassion and boldness.

As you sit in the church foyer during the meeting, the fallen elder's wife walks in, obviously distraught and shaken. You greet her, and she pours out the whole story in a flood of tears. You embrace her and let her cry on your shoulder. Other elders' wives arrive, and you offer comfort and reassurance to them. You are primarily there for your husband, but you eagerly meet the needs of others in your peripheral vision.

Jesus was the master of acute peripheral vision. On his way to heal Jairus's gravely ill daughter, a woman with a chronic hemorrhage touched his robe (see Mark 5). Jesus broke stride long enough to turn to her and deal with her need before moving on with the distraught father.

Can you imagine Jairus's thoughts when Jesus stopped to heal the woman? Here is Jairus, leading Jesus through the crowd, knowing that only Jesus can save his little girl, who is at death's door. Then suddenly Jesus stops to tend to a bleeding woman. Perhaps Jairus thinks, *Not now, Jesus. I'm afraid there won't be time. My little girl is dying. Why are you wasting time on that woman? Please come now! Please hurry!*

Then, as Jesus miraculously heals the woman, Jairus's worst fears are realized. News reaches him that his daughter has died. Jesus ignores the sad news. Instead, he tells the grieving father, "Don't be afraid. Just trust me" (Mark 5:36). Can you sense the impact those words must have had in Jairus's heart?

Jairus *did* trust Jesus, and his daughter was raised from the dead. Jesus kept his focus on ministering to Jairus and his daughter. But that did not keep him from ministering to a bleeding woman on the periphery.

Even on the way to his death on Golgotha, carrying his own cross, Jesus stopped to minister to some weeping women along the path. He is our example of being focused on what is most important while keeping an eye out for others who need us. You can minister first to your spouse while being alert to others nearby in need: your children, your parents, your coworkers, fellow church members, and others.

Often it is enough for others simply to know that you notice them and acknowledge their need. They know that they have not been ignored. Then assure them that you will follow through on their need or request. It might sound like this: "Jason, I know you need to talk about this, and I want to hear about it too. But I have to talk to your mom right now, and I promise I'll be down with you in about ten minutes, okay?" or, "Honey, I can't deal with that on the phone right now. I have to meet with someone here in just a moment. Let's go out for dessert tonight and talk it through. Will that be all right?"

You are not trying to get rid of people who need you with statements like these. Rather, you are assuring them of your interest and commitment while trying to control the timing of your helpful actions. But you must follow through with these appointments. Without follow-through, you send the message that you can't be trusted, which always damages a relationship.

Practice Relational Triage

On the battlefield or the site of a major disaster, medical personnel divide casualties into three groups: the dying, the seriously wounded, and the superficially wounded. They know they have little chance of saving the dying, and care for the superficially wounded can be delayed. So it is the seriously wounded who receive immediate attention.

This is a helpful way to look at the people problems in your life. Who is the most seriously wounded person in your circle of relationships today? Who genuinely needs you the most? Whose pain must be addressed to prevent more serious damage? For example, meeting your daughter's need for affirmation by attending her piano recital may not be as critical as rushing to help your sister who has just been in a car accident. Attending a committee meeting at church is not as important as staying home with a child who has just been kicked off a school team.

Maintain your priorities of meeting your own basic needs and the needs of your spouse. But keep an eye out for the needy others on the periphery, especially those who are in dangerous or painful situations.

JESUS CHRIST, OUR EXAMPLE

Think again about Jesus' leading Jairus through the crowds, hastening to the man's home to heal his daughter. The Master stopped to meet the immediate need of the bleeding woman. Why? Because she reached out to him, and he responded with his deep love and care for her.

People in your life today, perhaps a number of them, are reaching out for your attention and care. They are hurting, and they need or want something from you to relieve the pain. If you feel like exploding under the pressure of people in crisis or just running away, don't be embarrassed. It's a normal response.

Gary and I encourage you to take a deep breath, say a prayer, and then follow Jesus' example. Do what you can to help. You don't have to do it perfectly, just willingly. And if you and your spouse are in a conflict right now, you need to start at home. That's your priority. You may need to say something like, "Honey, I know we're struggling to connect these days. There is so much going on, and I feel overwhelmed by it. But I don't want to shut you out. I know you need to hear what I'm thinking and feeling, and I want to hear what's going on in your heart. You are my partner, and we need to be on the same team."

Occasional confrontations like these may be difficult, but they can also be some of the richest times in marriage and family life. The very stresses that divide us can also push us into closer relationship with our spouses. It's vital that you build the castle of your marriage relationship on the rock of healthy communication, deep respect, and mutual commitment.

People pressures will never go away in this lifetime. But you can guard your heart, guard your spouse, and guard your home against their harmful effects. As you exercise guarding love in your many relationships, beginning at home, you will notice a difference in how people respond to you.

Let's bring this chapter home to *your* home. Where are relationship pressures taking a toll on your marriage and family? What are one or two things you can do to make an impact on your family by reorienting your approach to those pressures? Does your spouse need you to step closer with reassurance that you are in the same boat with him or her? Perhaps one of your kids or grandkids need to be reminded that you are there for them and willing to walk through a pressure-packed situation. Or maybe you need to invite someone into the boat with you. We need each other, folks. Let's be God with skin on to those who matter the most.

Chapter Six

PRONE TO WANDER

We BEGIN THIS CHAPTER WITH FOUR BRIEF STORIES THAT ALERT us to another serious threat to a divorce-proof marriage. Barb will tell you about Pam and Sherry, then I will relate my encounters with Roger and Stan.

※

Pam is the typical "Minivan Mama." Pam's day is filled with running the kids to and from school, lessons, team practice, and shopping. She is on the PTA board and serves faithfully as a homeroom mother. Stu, her husband, works long hours just to make the mortgage payments and provide a comfortable life for his family. Pam and Stu are also very involved in their little church.

As with many busy young couples, much of the freshness and excitement has been squeezed out of Pam and Stu's marriage by their frantic daily schedule. There is little time left in the day for quiet conversation, and they have little energy left at night for back rubs, tender touches, and romance in the bedroom. Boredom has crept into their relationship, but they call it being too busy. Gary and I have seen it too many times in countless marriages. Busyness plus boredom is often a recipe for marital disaster.

One Saturday morning at the mall, while Stu was baby-sitting at home, Pam ran into Alex, an old boyfriend from college. Just seeing him sparked memories of their past romance, and the feelings caught her off guard. Alex complimented her looks and poured on the charm, just like always. Pam found herself loving it. As they chatted, she tried to use logic to fight off the feelings welling inside her. *All the man I ever wanted is at home,* she thought. *Stu is just as charming and romantic; he's just a little rusty. And he thinks I'm beautiful too; he just hasn't said it for a while.*

When Alex asked for her phone number, Pam knew she should say no. But she couldn't do it. So she gave him her number—not her home number, but her personal cell number. Alex said he would call. Pam secretly hoped he would.

Sherry loved to sing, especially for the choir director, Jay. His good looks and great personality coupled with his strong spiritual side were very attractive to her. She was embarrassed by her own giddiness whenever she talked with him. She felt like a schoolgirl experiencing her first crush.

But Sherry was married. Her husband, Phil, was a good man, and he worked hard. But he wasn't as communicative and outgoing as Jay was. Sherry's fascination with the choir director continued to grow. He seemed to enjoy her good-natured bantering, which further weakened her resolve. She couldn't help flirting with him. Jay appeared not to regard her as a flirt, which only intrigued Sherry more. What began as a secret admiration was now occupying her thoughts. She lived for choir practice, and she anticipated chance meetings with Jay at church or in the community. Sherry didn't know what she would do if he returned her interest.

Roger, an executive in a large corporation, had received national recognition for his work. He had a nice family and a sterling reputation in the community. When I traveled to his part of the country, he generously agreed to meet with me and give me a little career counseling.

During the two-hour meeting in his plush office, my eyes kept wandering to a large, elegantly framed print mounted on the wall behind his desk. You may have seen the picture. It shows a fiftysomething executive sitting in his office speaking with a visitor across the desk. The visitor is Jesus Christ. The executive seems to be talking about the complexities and problems of his business, and Christ is listening compassionately.

The message of the picture was eloquent, and I have never forgotten it. We need to live as if Jesus Christ is visibly present in our study, our office, or our home. I was deeply impressed that a man of Roger's stature and influence would display such a painting in his office for everyone to see. I remember thinking, *Maybe someday I will be this secure in my faith.*

Several years later, a friend told me that Roger had become involved in an adulterous relationship with a customer, a woman he spent time with in that same office, right under the picture of Jesus Christ. Their office meetings led to hotel encounters and ultimately to the dissolution of both of their marriages. Roger also lost his business, all the trappings of his success, and his Christian testimony. I cannot help but wonder what happened to the painting that so captivated me.

When Stan walked into my office for a counseling appoinent, I knew he was in some kind of deep trouble. His face was ashen.

He was obviously shaken. I took a deep breath, lifted a silent prayer, and asked him to sit down.

"I didn't think it could ever happen, Gary," Stan began. "Natalie and I were just friends. She was going through a hard time in her marriage when I met her at work."

I sighed deeply. I already knew where this conversation was going.

"Nothing happened at first," he continued. "We would have lunch together at work occasionally. She talked about how things were going in her marriage, and I found myself opening up about Susan and the hassles I was having at home. And Natalie really cared. She was interested in what I was saying. Susan and I used to have that kind of chemistry, but over the years of paying bills and raising kids, I guess we lost it. Natalie awakened all kinds of desires in me.

"Our lunches became longer—two hours, three hours—and we had such a good time together. From there it got out of hand so fast that I can't believe it. From lunches to meetings after work, from longing looks to tender touches. Our first time together in a hotel seemed so natural. My body was raging with desire, and I couldn't think of anything else but being with her. I was like a runaway freight train."

"Does Susan know about Natalie?" I asked.

"Yeah, Susan knows," Stan sighed, his face clouded with sadness. "She wants to take the kids and leave. I can't believe this is happening. If only I could go back. If only I hadn't let this thing get started. I didn't mean to hurt anyone."

Barb and I cannot count the number of Stans, Rogers, Sherrys, and Pams we have encountered in our ministry of divorce-proofing America's marriages. We have heard their sad stories in the counseling office, on our radio program, and at our marriage conferences. These stories all begin innocently enough: a mild attraction to another man, a second glance at another woman, a sharing of marital problems with a "concerned friend" of the opposite sex. But unguarded hearts are vulnerable to uncontrolled attractions and passions. And soon a marriage is sullied and two lives—and usually more—are scarred by an emotional affair or illicit sexual interlude.

One of the most subtle and potentially destructive threats to your marriage comes in the form of sexual temptation. We use the word *subtle* because it is rare to hear of someone being overtly and purposely seduced by a person other than his or her spouse. The enemy of your heart and home doesn't really need a gaping opening like that to ignite temptation. All he needs is a moment of unguarded fascination or attraction, a few unbridled thoughts about *what if?* Like a cancer, small impure thoughts can grow into a disease that will threaten the life of your marriage relationship.

Men and women are often drawn into marital infidelity differently. For men, the attraction is largely physical. Typically, men are captivated by the sight or thought of a woman's body or fantasies of how she would be in bed, as compared to his wife. For women, the temptation is more emotional, being lured into a relationship by a man's kindness, attentiveness, or affection, as compared to her husband's. These traits are not mutually exclusive, however; women are also attracted to men they consider handsome or virile, and men are attracted to women who are attentive and caring.

In this chapter we will address physical and emotional involvement separately. I will talk about the dangers of sexual temptation from a man's perspective. Barb will address a woman's unique temptations. But don't read the section just for your gender. You also need to know what kinds of sexual temptation your husband or wife is facing. Besides, you will identify with both traits because you are both physical and emotional beings. Then, in the last section of the chapter, Barb and I will coach you on ways to guard your heart and marriage against this insidious threat.

THE PERILS OF PHYSICAL INVOLVEMENT

Recent research indicates that men are stepping into adultery at astronomical rates. According to Maggie Scarf, author of *Intimate Partners,* "Most experts do consider the 'educated guess' that at the present time some 50 to 65 percent of husbands and 45 to 55 percent of wives become extramaritally involved by the age of forty to be a relatively sound and reasonable one."[1]

This means that for every ten guys you see at work, in your neighborhood, or in your Sunday school class, five to six of them have been unfaithful to their wives at some point in their lives. About half of all men are living in an adulterous relationship, have left their marriages because of adultery, or are currently trying to rebuild the marital trust crippled by an affair.

There's no denying it: Men are acutely vulnerable to sexual temptation. We are wired with sex on our minds much of the day. As we discovered in a survey for our book *The Five Love Needs of Men and Women,* one of a man's greatest needs is for the sexual love of his wife. So where do you think Satan will attack a man to make him stumble and fall into sexual sin? That's why men are quick to notice a pretty face, a shapely figure, a little too much exposed skin, or a flirtatious wink—and then look again.

In reality, "falling" into adultery rarely happens for men or women. Illicit liaisons don't just pop up out of nowhere. They grow out of something that was once innocent and harmless. And healthy marriages don't just go bad overnight. They erode over time through neglect and disinterest. Stan said his affair felt like a runaway freight train. In truth, it took some time for that train to build up momentum, and he had done nothing to slow it down. The time to stop a train, of course, is when it's just getting started—that first furtive look, that first impure thought, that first inappropriate word or touch.

No, adultery doesn't begin in the perfumed darkness of a hotel room, in a secluded storeroom at the office, or in someone else's bedroom. It doesn't even begin with the first look or word or touch. For men and women, adultery begins in the heart. And for men particularly, it begins when the heart is not guarded against what the eyes see and what the mind fantasizes.

Why are men—Christians leaders, your friends, even your family members—tumbling into sexual sin? Why does adultery claim so many men? Consider Solomon's words in Proverbs: "The lips of an immoral woman are as sweet as honey, and her mouth is smoother than oil" (5:3).

Who is this smooth, sweet woman? Solomon is writing about a prostitute. Most of you men would say, "Hey, Gary, I would *never* go to a prostitute." True, but think about the basic characteristics of a prostitute. She is enticing. She knows how to catch your eye and turn your head. She knows all the sensual moves. She knows how to hook a man. This could be your next-door neighbor, a woman in your church, your coworker, your wife's friend, your buddy's wife—any woman who crosses your path. Or it could be the image of a woman on a computer screen or an airbrushed image in a magazine.

Solomon continues: "But the result is as bitter as poison, sharp as a double-edged sword. Her feet go down to death; her steps lead straight to the grave. For she does not care about the path to life. She staggers down a crooked trail and doesn't even realize where it leads" (Proverbs 5:4-6).

Quite a transformation: sweet honey to bitter poison, smooth oil to a sword, a garden path of sensual delights to a dead-end road. Solomon warns us about the consequences of sexual sin. A man not only runs the risk of contracting a sexual disease and killing his marriage, but he also forms a physical and emotional bond that will damage him and the woman he is with. When a man goes to bed with another woman, he is not only acting selfishly and wounding his own soul and marriage; he is also wounding the woman he is with, soiling her marriage or the future marriage God may be preparing her for. The damage is incalculable.

Solomon goes on: "Run from her! Don't go near the door of her house! If you do, you will lose your honor and hand over to merciless people everything you have achieved in life. Strangers will obtain your wealth, and someone else will enjoy the fruit of your labor" (Proverbs 5:8-10).

Men, that's a very steep price to pay for taking a longer look at your coworker's figure, fantasizing about making love to your wife's best friend, flipping through a pornographic magazine, or scrolling through an Internet Web site. Guard your heart against these physical temptations, and you will guard your wife and your marriage against grievous pain.

Now let's look at the issue of sexual temptation from the woman's perspective. Barb will provide some helpful insight.

THE PERILS OF EMOTIONAL ATTACHMENT

For women as well as men, adultery begins in the heart. But as Gary mentioned, a woman is more likely to be tempted sexually on the emotional level. There is certainly a physical attraction, but it is usually the accompanying emotional attachment that leads a woman into an adulterous affair. She is lured away by a man's tenderness, openness, warmth, personality, and attentiveness, even when these qualities are genuine and not put on to catch a woman.

Women, do you feel an emotional flutter when a certain man—not your husband—walks into the room? Do you feel a little light-headed when he looks you in the eye and hangs on every word you say? Do you feel like a schoolgirl with a crush when he comments on how sharp you look or asks if you have lost weight? These experiences may be the first entrapping tentacles that, if you grant them full access to your heart, could ruin your marriage.

When you sense that someone else is captivating your heart in some way, when this attraction results in increased disappointment or frustration toward your husband or when you begin to dwell on or act out your fascination, it is time to confront the threat. It's not too late, but it's late enough. Here are several steps you can take to stop an affair before it starts.

Admit to yourself and confess to God that you are tantalized by this temptation. There is no safer place on earth than going to God and agreeing with him over the thoughts and feelings you have been keeping secret. When we deny or bury our issues, they are not dead; they are just buried alive and will continue to torment us. Get free by surrendering whatever secret thought or fantasy you have been clutching.

Confront the lies you are believing. Put a stop to any of these common lies and partial truths—or others like them—you have been entertaining:

- ⊕ His attention makes me feel good, and it's not hurting anyone.
- ⊕ There's a connection. He really understands me.
- ⊕ I can talk to him about everything. He always makes time for me.

⊕ I can see myself ending up with him.

⊕ I can tell he is attracted to me.

⊕ I think he has feelings for me.

Replace the lies with truth. Get into the Word of God, and search for verses that apply to guarding your heart and mind against sexual temptation. Write these verses on index cards, and carry them with you. Read them often, or memorize them. Whenever you feel your thoughts slipping, pull out a card and read it. Soon God's truth will fill the void of the lies you have dismissed and empower you against lies in the future. Here are some Scripture passages I recommend for breaking free of captivity: 1 Corinthians 6:13-15,18-20; Ephesians 5:3; Colossians 3:5-8,12; 1 Thessalonians 4:3-5, 7.

Receive God's grace, and draw the line. When God washes away all your mistakes, you can make a new beginning. You don't ever have to return to your former ways of viewing other men or responding to them. But you do have to make some strong decisions about the future. You decide that, with God's strength, you will not allow the enemy to gain a foothold. Temptation will always be just a look, a thought, a smile, or a conversation away. So guard your heart against it. Some additional Scripture verses I recommend for experiencing freedom are these: Proverbs 4:23; Isaiah 1:18; 1 Corinthians 10:12; Galatians 5:16-18; Ephesians 4:22-24.

Sometimes a woman is drawn away by the attention and interest of other men because her husband is *not* paying attention to her and *not* interested in her. Lisa called in to our daily radio program for advice. She told us, "I am married and a Christian, but I can't help seeking the attention of other men. I feel out of control because I really like the attention I receive, but it's getting me into trouble. How do I stop?"

As we talked to her, Lisa revealed that her problem started when her husband quit trying in their marriage and failed to meet Lisa's legitimate need for emotional closeness and intimacy. When a man stops pursuing and courting his wife, her heart is left unattended and vulnerable to any other man who shows interest in her. Lisa didn't want to stop because the attentions of other men were like a drug that soothed the pain of her difficult marriage.

However, a disinterested and inattentive husband is no excuse for a woman to turn to other men to meet her emotional needs. It will only make a bad situation worse and ultimately more painful. If you are living in a situation like Lisa's, invest your prayers and efforts into trying to make your own marriage better.

Like Pam at the beginning of this chapter, Rebecca found herself swamped by the care of her young family. She was also frustrated that her husband, Bob, was working so many hours and not giving her the attention she desired. One day her neighbor Sid happened to be in his backyard while she was doing some gardening. They stopped to chat, and Sid complimented Rebecca about her beautiful yard and hard work. She felt flattered at being appreciated and listened to. It was like water to a thirsty plant.

But a few mornings later, Rebecca woke up realizing she had been dreaming about Sid. It shocked her because she knew her heart wasn't right. It was time to put things on the table with her husband. So she sat down with Bob and told him she needed more time with him for conversation. She admitted that her emotional connection with him was strained and that she had been avoiding him sexually. She humbly and gently took responsibility for her actions and apologized for slighting him.

Her words began to melt the wall between them and opened

the door for his confession. He had been angry and frustrated because she had been cool toward him in bed. He admitted his neglect and lack of loving care. They embraced each other and decided to place new boundaries around their marriage, guarding their hearts with mutual respect and care.

Rebecca and Bob's marriage was revolutionized. They now hold each other accountable for their actions. They work at anticipating and meeting each other's needs. They are free from the secret hurts of the past and committed not to repeat them.

What can you do to maximize your resistance to sexual temptation? Gary will share with you several guardrails to keep your life on the road to faithfulness.

GUARDRAILS TO FAITHFULNESS

You probably wouldn't travel a steep, winding mountain road in your car if there weren't guardrails for safety. Guardrails are there for a purpose: to protect you and your car from plunging over the edge.

In the same way, you need to establish guardrails in your life to keep you safe from the sexual temptations you will encounter on your journey. The following four guardrails will help you guard your heart and marriage from the perils and pain of unfaithfulness.

A Strong Relationship with the Father

Look at the opening words in Solomon's warning against sexual temptation: "My son, pay attention to my wisdom; listen carefully to my wise counsel. Then you will learn to be discreet and will store up knowledge" (Proverbs 5:1-2). The wise king urged his son to heed his wisdom and counsel in order to learn discretion and be knowledgeable in the area of moral and sexual behavior. We also need wisdom and counsel, but not just from a wise, earthly father. We need the insight of the wisest Father of all.

Your ongoing intimate relationship with Father God is your strongest guardrail against sexual temptation. He has the best counsel. He knows exactly how men and women are wired—because he wired us. How you deal with your sexuality is of the utmost importance to God. The closer you stay to him, the greater will be your access to his wisdom and counsel for resisting sexual temptation.

One way you tap into God's wisdom is to pay attention to and obey his Word. He instructs us through the apostle Paul: "Fix your thoughts on what is true and honorable and right. Think about things that are pure and lovely and admirable. Think about things that are excellent and worthy of praise" (Philippians 4:8). This is wise counsel. Inviting God to examine and direct our thoughts will always push us toward purity. Your interaction with God and his Word will weave a web of discipline and protection around your most private thoughts.

A Cautious Relationship with Others of the Opposite Sex

The runaway freight train Stan described in his sad story began with carelessness in his relationship with Natalie. He allowed himself to get too close emotionally and then physically. The same was true with Pam and Sherry. They did not establish a guardrail of respectful relational distance between themselves and the men who captured their attention. We're not talking about cutting off all contact with the opposite sex. We're talking about being cautious and alert for temptation in these relationships and maintaining a margin of distance that will help you resist those temptations. Here are several practical tips.

Dismiss and replace tempting thoughts. Don't allow any unwholesome thoughts to make a home in your mind. *Wow, what a figure!* or *He has such a cute smile and sparkling personality* or *I'll bet she keeps her husband happy* or *I could sit and talk with him for hours.* If thoughts like these pop into your head, it's time to look away or leave the room. If you can't leave, shift your focus away from that person by thinking of your spouse. Start praying for your spouse and your kids. And pray for the other person's family. Pray for his or her relationship with God. Wrong sexual thoughts don't easily coexist with sincere prayer.

Don't gaze too long into the windows of the soul. Eye contact in a conversation is good. But if you catch a look that is too intense, too engaging, or makes you uncomfortable, avert your eyes and resist that gaze. When I am speaking with a woman, I purposely avoid consistent eye contact with her. I know that a deep gaze can stir something in one or both of us, something I don't want stirred up. I don't turn away because I have to; I turn away because I have the privilege of saving that eye contact for one woman: my dear one, Barb.

Don't go out of your way to see or meet someone. Don't take a different hallway back to your office just to encounter that attractive new employee. Don't select a seat in church because it is near that person who loves to talk to you after the service. Don't linger after a meeting hoping to be noticed by that certain person. You get the idea. And don't meet with a tempting person privately, even if the purpose is legitimate. Invite your spouse to come along, meet with a larger group, or meet in a public place where you are never alone.

Be careful with physical touch. Growing up, my family was very affectionate, and physical touch is important to me in a relationship. I like to shake my buddies' hands, slap their backs, and sometimes give them a manly bear hug. And I'm affectionate with Barb and our kids all the time. But I use a different standard when I'm with other women. No matter how affectionate you are at home, you also need a different standard with members of the opposite sex, even persons you know well and greatly respect. Here's a helpful question to ask yourself: If your spouse, your children, your mother, and Jesus were in the room watching you give that hug or pat, would they heartily approve? If not, don't do it.

Bottom line, men, physical purity begins with and stands on your relationship to the Lord. If you want to leave a godly life story for your children and grandchildren, you need to be wide open to God's invasion of your heart and mind. Continually ask yourself these kinds of questions:

⊕ Are my actions honoring God, my spouse, or myself?
⊕ Do my actions or words even hint of anything that may dishonor my wife?
⊕ Are my selfish actions or words opening a Pandora's box that will disgrace my children?

Psalm 139:23-24 beautifully expresses an honest admission of every man and woman's need to stay honest and clean before God: "Search me, O God, and know my heart; test me and know my thoughts. Point out anything in me that offends you, and lead me along the path of everlasting life."

Keep conversation general. Many, many affairs are started or fueled when a man and woman who are not married to each other talk about their personal lives. Talk about the weather, your work, the team, the new pastor, the news, and the like. But if the other person starts sharing something of a personal nature— even if disguising it as a "prayer request"—redirect or terminate the conversation.

When all else fails, run for your moral life. If for some reason you find yourself in a compromising situation with someone of the opposite sex, immediately and physically remove yourself from that situation. You don't have to explain or apologize. And don't let the other person convince you it's no big deal. Never try to negotiate with the devil. Do what Joseph in the Old Testament did when Potiphar's wife attempted to seduce him: drop everything and run (see Genesis 39).

An Open Relationship with Other Christians
Your Christian friends can also be a trustworthy guardrail of sexual purity in your life. Men, do you have a small circle of guys you can be brutally honest with about your struggles, men who will pray with you, check up on you, encourage you, and hold you accountable? Women, do you have a group of women who know your weaknesses and with whom you remain completely open, trusting them to tell you the truth to keep you from stumbling? You must be willing to lay aside anything that would hinder or rob you from allowing those people who know and love you to scrutinize your life. When you are defensive, proud, or resistant to be examined, you miss out on the opportunity to further your spiritual development. James admonishes, "Confess your sins to each other and pray for each other so that you may be healed. The earnest prayer of a righteous person has great power and wonderful results" (James 5:16).

We need a cadre of trustworthy Christian friends to encourage us to remain pure. We need good friends to edify us when we are struggling with sin in our lives. And we need good friends who can help restore us to obedience when we have stepped over the line in some way. If you don't have a group like this, find one or start one yourself. If the group you're in is all fun and games, change groups or suggest a Bible study on moral purity. Insist on a time of personal sharing and prayer during each meeting. You will be amazed at how thoughts of this group will intrude your thoughts during a moment of temptation.

A Fulfilling Relationship with Your Spouse

Solomon's words in Proverbs 5:15-19 are slanted to a husband, but you wives can make an appropriate translation: "Let your wife be a fountain of blessing for you. Rejoice in the wife of your youth. She is a loving doe, a graceful deer. Let her breasts satisfy you always. May you always be captivated by her love" (vv. 18-19).

In other words, if you are emotionally or sexually thirsty, head for your own well, the well God has provided for you. Quench your thirst at your own fountain instead of roaming around looking for another. And make sure you anticipate and meet your spouse's sexual needs. When you are full and satisfied sexually in your relationship with your spouse, neither of you will need to look elsewhere for satisfaction.

Also bring your emotional and relational needs to your spouse for fulfillment. Talk about your struggles, your dreams, your needs, your frustrations, and your joys from all levels of your life. Pray with each other. Laugh with each other. Cry with each other. Grieve with each other. Enjoy each other. Challenge each other. This is what intimacy is all about—sharing your innermost thoughts, feelings, desires, and drives with one another. Intimacy with your dear spouse will help keep you in the center of the road, even when other guardrails are missing.

A GOAL OF NO REGRETS

Let's turn to Solomon for one parting look at the outcome of a heart unguarded from sexual temptation: "Afterward you will groan in anguish when disease consumes your body, and you will say, 'How I hated discipline! If only I had not demanded my own way! Oh, why didn't I listen to my teachers? Why didn't I pay attention to those who gave me instruction? I have come to the brink of utter ruin, and now I must face public disgrace' " (Proverbs 5:11-14).

Can you imagine the pain experienced by a man like Stan who is on the brink of losing his family because of a sexual fling with a coworker? Or think how badly Roger felt seeing his family, business, and testimony go up in smoke because he did not guard against sexual temptation with a customer. Consider Rebecca's grief and remorse had she not put a stop to wrong thoughts about her neighbor.

Let's take it to another level. Visualize your spouse finding you in bed with another man or woman. How would you feel? Imagine confessing to your children that you had been unfaithful to their father or mother. Can you see the look of betrayal on their faces? What would you give never to have those experiences? How much would you pay for a life of no regrets with regard to your moral purity?

No amount of money can buy back the trust, intimacy, and innocence lost through sexual immorality. But you don't have to pay a cent to prevent an affair in your marriage. Simply add to the previous guardrails a goal for a life of no regrets when it comes to your sexual life. Decide now to guard your heart against anything that would cause you or your spouse such grief and pain in your marriage relationship.

If you have already fallen to temptation in this area, do something about it now. It may be too late to escape the hurt and distress you have caused. But you can begin to make things right and heal the wounds. Break off the relationship you are in. Confess to God and to your spouse. Seek counseling, and submit yourself to mature Christians to monitor your restoration. God loves you, and he will walk you and your spouse through each step of the healing you need.

There is hope for you. There is forgiveness. God has the power you need to be all he has called you to be. And he can help you guard your heart against further regret.

Stay alert, and remember: A guarded heart helps build a divorce-proof marriage.

Chapter Seven

A CLOUDED VIEW OF SUCCESS

$\mathcal{L}$ILY IS A TIRELESS VOLUNTEER IN THE COMMUNITY AND HER church. She spends many hours each week serving at the pregnancy care center and in an AIDS hospice. Lily has chaired local fund-raising drives for a number of organizations. And if there is a community cause that impacts children or the elderly, she is there, ready to stuff envelopes, make phone calls, or coordinate a bake sale. When asked why she is so involved, Lily says simply, "As a Christian, I'm committed to making the world a better place."

Nobody does household finances like Kevin. As a postal carrier with a wife and four kids, he is driven to stretch their modest income. He keeps a detailed account of the family's income and expenses on spreadsheets. Budgeting down to the penny, Kevin will stay up half the night finding an error or balancing accounts. The criteria for all purchases is not how badly they need the item but whether he can squeeze it out of the budget. Kevin is very proud of the money he has saved the family.

Ellie has turned mothering into an art form. She has read all the latest Christian books on parenting, belongs to MOPS and various play groups, and is on a first-name basis with every pediatrician in the clinic. Desiring the best possible learning environment for her three children, Ellie is homeschooling them. She spends hours poring over curriculum samples and attends workshops whenever she can fit them in. Someday, when the kids are in college, she may get back to her advertising career. But not until she fulfills her goal of being the best mother she can be.

***

Donnie came out of seminary intent on pastoring the largest church in his denomination. He volunteered to start a church in the toughest district, the one his peers avoided, and moved there with his wife and two preschool sons. Eagerly diving into the work, Donnie put in twelve- to fourteen-hour days canvassing the neighborhood, talking to people on the street, passing out flyers, and transforming a vacant theater into a church building. His efforts paid off, and the church started to grow, fueling Donnie to work even harder. Three years later, Donnie had the largest church in the district, and denomination officials were eyeing him for one of their larger churches closer to headquarters.

***

Each of these people is a success story in the making. Lily almost sounds like another Mother Teresa, doesn't she? Kevin's ability to squeeze a nickel may someday make him a rich man. Ellie may someday take the trophy as mother of the decade. And Pastor Donnie may write the next best-selling book on church growth. Each of them has a clearly focused definition of success, and they're going for it. These four are merely representative of countless numbers of Christian husbands, wives, and parents who are driven by success in some way.

You have to admire their goals and tenacity. But the pursuit of success can come with a high price tag. For example, Lily's husband and kids despise her for being gone from home so much as she helps others. Kevin's kids think their dad is more concerned about the budget than about them. Ellie's lonely husband wonders what happened to the wife who once put him first in her life. And Donnie has two sons with severe behavior problems and a wife addicted to prescription drugs. By the time many individuals and couples like these get to my office for counseling, their "success" has already levied a burdensome tax of relational pain they may never be able to pay off.

Success within boundaries is a good thing. But success at all costs, no matter how you define success, is a serious threat to your marriage and family. Barb and I urge you to guard your heart against an unhealthy drive to succeed that distances you from your spouse and children. Barb will begin by discussing in detail the danger signs of an unbalanced emphasis on success in your relationships. Then I will direct you to an alternative to success that will strengthen and help divorce-proof family relationships.

WHAT ARE YOUR TERMS OF SUCCESS?

How do you define success? Your definition and the amount of energy you invest in making that definition a reality in your life are largely a product of your upbringing and our culture. Here are four popular and overlapping expressions of the drive to succeed in our world. Do you see yourself striding resolutely down any of these roads?

"I will be a success when I make my mark in the world." Success is often measured in terms of the contribution a person makes to society. Lily is driven to spend long hours as a volunteer, even at the expense of isolating herself from her family, in order to leave the world a better place. Others seek to leave monuments of achievement, such as a building, an institution, a fund or en-

dowment, legislation, an organization, or the like. Or the goal may be as down-to-earth as starting a profitable business or transforming your home into a decorating showcase.

In most cases, these contributions are good things, benefiting other people, relieving suffering, or even advancing the cause of Christ in some way. They become counterproductive when our dearest relationships are scarred as you make your mark.

"I will be a success when I am financially secure." Financial security is a relative thing. To Kevin the postman, it means making enough to live on while squirreling away enough for the kids' college education and his retirement. For others, financial security is measured in hundreds of thousands or millions of dollars. You may have a certain dollar figure in mind for the ultimate nest egg. No matter how golden that nest egg may be, if your drive to get it disrupts the other members of your nest, it's not worth it.

"I will be a success when I become the best at what I do." Only the most shortsighted and sedentary among us have no goals for improvement or advancement. And relatively few people are content to remain mediocre or average across the board. Don't we all yearn to be good, better, or the best at something? You may strive to be the top salesperson in the company, the first in your family to earn a million dollars, the best tennis player in your area, or, like Ellie, the best mother or father you can be. In the process of becoming the best, some, like Ellie, have alienated those dearest to them.

"I will be a success when I am somebody." Praise, respect, position, applause, fame, reputation—all are important to those striving to achieve success through fame. In what ways do you seek the spotlight of attention and recognition? Are you after an Oscar, a Nobel prize, the CEO's office? Or would you be satisfied just to be named president of your PTA, discussion leader in

your Bible study, or best actor at the amateur community theater? In your quest for recognition, don't forget to recognize and care for the dear ones of your family.

Even the drive to be somebody in the kingdom of God can be a deterrent to God's purposes. Just hours before their Master was crucified, the disciples were jockeying for key positions in Christ's kingdom (see Luke 22:24). Pastor Donnie was on the fast track to becoming the poster boy for his denomination, but he was neglecting his wife and sons to achieve his goal. Beware lest setting your sights on success lands you in the company of those Jesus identified this way: "For they loved human praise more than the praise of God" (John 12:43).

POTHOLES ON THE ROAD TO SUCCESS

How can you tell if your desire and drive for success have gone too far? Look for any of the following telltale signs in your life. These are the potholes on the road to success, and they can spoil everything. And if you can't see them, ask your spouse and your children if they see any of these traits in you.

Going for the Jugular

Competition is a part of life, and in its more positive forms, competition is good. I love it when grocery stores compete for my grocery budget with coupons, specials, and price wars. When employees are competing for top salesperson or employee-of-the-month awards, the result should be increased business and profits. Our kids compete for good grades and for positions on the school teams. Competition is healthy and beneficial when it stays within the bounds of fair play and good sportsmanship.

But we all know how we can get carried away in the heat of

competition, step over the edge, and go for the jugular. Where is the line? Here are a few examples:

- ⊕ One politician campaigns hard on his own merits and experience. Another politician runs an underhanded smear campaign against his opponent.
- ⊕ One mother coaches and encourages her daughter in a cheerleading competition. Another mother hires a hit man to kill her daughter's rival in the competition.
- ⊕ One athlete is out to defeat his opponent. Another athlete is out to injure his opponent in order to win.
- ⊕ One company invests in research and development, hoping to produce the best product on the market. Another company steals design secrets from its rival.

Does the intensity of your quest for success spur you to go for the jugular in the worst sense of the term, such as to hurt, to defame, or to embarrass your rival? Do your toes dangle over the line of indecency and dishonesty in the heat of the battle? Do you view and treat your rival as the enemy? Do you allow competition to bring out the worst in your emotions: anger, bitterness, revenge, hatred?

If the competition element in your drive to succeed turns you into some kind of a monster, it will likely poison your relationships at home. No prize is worth that steep a price.

High and Mighty

Naaman in the Bible was a proud man; he had the kind of pride that hardens the heart. As a courageous and successful military commander, he had what today's kids call an "attitude." Scripture calls it a proud heart. You can find his story in 2 Kings 5.

But Naaman had a problem: He was a leper. He wanted to be

healed of this loathsome disease, of course. But in his pride he wanted preferential treatment. Pride has a way of convincing us that we deserve extra attention and special treatment.

Naaman heard that Israel's prophet Elisha could cure him of his leprosy. So Naaman went to Elisha's house. Elisha sent a messenger to say to him, "Go and wash yourself seven times in the Jordan River. Then your skin will be restored, and you will be healed of leprosy" (v. 10).

The proud warrior was miffed—for several reasons. First, Elisha didn't even come out to talk to him; he sent a servant. Second, instead of just making Naaman well on the spot, Elisha told him to dip in the Jordan seven times. Third, he was sent to the small, dirty Jordan River. Naaman's first response was to stomp off in a huff. Eventually, however, he humbled himself and obeyed Elisha's commands to the letter, and he was healed of leprosy. He had to stoop very low to find the door to his healing and a relationship with Elisha's God. All his success and his attitude of pride got him nowhere.

One of the great temptations of success is the big head and hard heart of pride. In your drive for success, or in the successes you have already achieved, do you see yourself as just a bit more special than the next person? Do you expect—and think you deserve—preferential treatment? Do you find yourself butting heads with God, your spouse, your children, and others because they don't jump to your tune? Pride will eventually make your success hollow and push your family away from you.

Enough Is Never Enough

Success is satisfying. It feels good to reach a goal, make a big sale, finish a long project, or see your kids excel in school as a result of your tutoring. But sometimes you may look around and see that your achievement wasn't as great as someone else's. You built up your Bible study group to twenty, but Sue's group has grown to thirty in the same time. You helped your kids memorize ten Bible verses over the summer, but your neighbor's kids memorized eighteen verses. You achieved the salesperson-of-the-month award, but your coworker earned the salesperson-of-the-year award. Suddenly your success seems shallow and unsatisfying. You want more. You want what they have.

That's called envy, and it is another pothole on the road to success. To the envious, enough is not good enough if someone else has more. Proverbs 14:30 says, "A heart at peace gives life to the body, but envy rots the bones" (NIV). Your dissatisfaction with the success you have achieved and your envy of others' success will make life unpleasant for those closest to you.

Envy's first cousin is greed, the thirst for more than you need, more than you can use, more than you can handle. Solomon writes, "A greedy man brings trouble to his family" (Proverbs 15:27, NIV). No wonder the apostle Paul instructs us, "Don't be greedy for the good things of this life, for that is idolatry" (Colossians 3:5).

The opposite of envy and greed is contentment. When you are content at each stage on the road to success, you are at peace—and so are the others around you. Solomon tells us in Proverbs 4:25-27, "Look straight ahead, and fix your eyes on what lies before you. Mark out a straight path for your feet; then stick to the path and stay safe. Don't get sidetracked; keep your feet from following evil." Pursuing success will be a benefit for your family if you fix your gaze on what you hope to attain, not on what others have attained.

Under the Weight of Worry

Linda's definition of success is getting back to her wedding-day weight of 136 pounds. Her love for burgers, fries, and milk shakes during the nine years of her marriage to Tom have caused her to slide over the 200-pound mark. Linda knows Tom loves her unconditionally, and he never bugs her about her weight. But she wants nothing more than to fit into her wedding gown for their tenth anniversary.

So she launches into a strict plan of diet and exercise. Every day she measures grams and counts calories—then measures and counts again. *Did I get the numbers right?* she worries. *If I mess up the count, I won't reach my goal.* Doubtful that the plan will really work, she dumps it and starts another, then another.

Concerned that she might binge on the wrong foods, Linda will not buy anything that isn't dietetic. Tom and the kids are sick of rice cakes and fat-free salad dressing. Paranoid that she might go off her diet at a restaurant, she refuses to go out to eat with Tom. Worried that she isn't getting her heart rate high enough, Linda goes to the gym twice a day—every day. Her whole life is consumed with her goal, but it's driving the family crazy.

Whatever success you hope to gain is diminished and devalued if you worry yourself sick over it. Worry pulls you away from trust and obedience to God. Worry is a distrust of God's resources and an attempt to live by your own devices. And when worry has you tied up in knots, you can bet your family, like Linda's, isn't having much fun.

Jesus said, "Don't worry about everyday life—whether you have enough food, drink, and clothes. Doesn't life consist of more than food and clothing? Look at the birds. They don't need to plant or harvest or put food in barns because your heavenly Father feeds them. And you are far more valuable to him than they are. Can all your worries add a single moment to your life? Of course not" (Matthew 6:25-27). The apostle Paul expressed a similar warning: "Don't worry about anything; instead, pray about everything. Tell God what you need, and thank him for all he has done" (Philippians 4:6). Success isn't worth worrying about, to you or to your family.

Instead of beating yourself up trying to climb to the pinnacle of success in your life, there is a healthier and more rewarding way to make your mark in the world. Gary will coach you on shifting your gaze from success to significance.

REWARDS ON THE ROAD TO SIGNIFICANCE

King Solomon tried to fill his ego needs through his compulsive lifestyle. The man had it all. He was a king, an author, a builder, a diplomat, a trader, a patron of the arts, and a collector. Yet in spite of all the wisdom God gave him, Solomon turned away from the Lord in his frenetic search for happiness and fulfillment. He lived life with his foot to the floorboard and every fantasy at his fingertips. Yet he remains one of the most graphic scriptural examples of a man steeped in regret, profound pain, and remorse. His summary is depressing: "So now I hate life because everything done here under the sun is so irrational. Everything is meaningless, like chasing the wind" (Ecclesiastes 2:17).

Solomon concludes that the more we emphasize human success, the more harried our lives become for us and those around us. But he has a solution. The final verses of Ecclesiastes read: "Here is my final conclusion: Fear God and obey his commands, for this is the duty of every person. God will judge us for everything we do, including every secret thing, whether good or bad" (Ecclesiastes 12:13-14). The more we emphasize our relationship with God, the more we will be fulfilled and content, helping to make life bearable and even enjoyable for our spouse and family.

The Success of Significance

Barb and I call this a life of significance. On the surface, success and significance may seem like synonyms, but they really are not. For example, you can achieve great success in life—a six- or seven-figure income, perfectly obedient children, or similar accomplishments—without achieving meaning and significance. Ask Solomon. And you can enjoy a life of significance in terms of your relationship and service to God and others without achieving success by the world's definition. Furthermore, if you spend your life frantically trying to make your mark, secure financial independence, or attract fame, you may leave your family in the dust. But if you devote yourself to a life of spiritual and eternal significance, your quest by its very nature will include and nurture your spouse and children. Pursue significance, and you will guard your heart and home against the threat of the drive for success.

Success is fleeting. Significance—our standing with God and everything we do in his name—lasts forever. When you temper your success with a goal of significance, you can still find fulfillment and achievement in life while paying attention to matters of the heart. You can still make your mark while keeping your personal growth and relationships intact.

We need to redefine success in terms of significance. True success is not only a matter of money, achievement, or position but also of compassion, kindness, courage, generosity, and love. True success is an issue of character, not performance. It's an issue of being the person, spouse, and parent God designed you to be, not of how much money you can earn or how nice your house is.

Who makes us significant? Significance comes from Jesus Christ. He created us in order to glorify himself. That's our primary mission in life, to bring honor and glory to Christ. He is the

One who makes us significant. Our performance or what others think about us pales in comparison to what God thinks about us. The apostle Paul put it this way: "I'm not trying to be a people pleaser! No, I am trying to please God. If I were still trying to please people, I would not be Christ's servant" (Galatians 1:10).

Sure, we care what others think about us. But it's not everything, not all-important. Yes, we want others to like us and respect us, but not at the cost of our integrity. Our worth and significance are determined by the person of Jesus Christ. When we reflect him in our lives as spouses and parents, we are fulfilling his plan for us.

Achieving Significance by Not Achieving

Christ makes us significant, but how do we flesh out true significance in everyday life? What is our part? Significance is not anything we can do; rather it is based on simple trust in Christ. Scripture says we need to have the faith of a little child.

Think about the kinds of people who surrounded the Lord Jesus during the latter days of his earthly ministry. The scribes and teachers of the law were posturing and strutting their knowledge, their righteous performance, and their flashy Hebrew credentials. The Pharisees made sure everyone knew how important they were not only by the way they dressed, prayed, and gave alms but also by the deference and respect they demanded from everyone else. Even the Lord's own disciples nursed visions of future greatness and argued among themselves over who would be most significant in the coming messianic kingdom.

About that time the Lord gave them all an object lesson they would never forget. He invited a little child into their midst and said, "I assure you, unless you turn from your sins and become as little children, you will never get into the Kingdom of

Heaven. Therefore, anyone who becomes as humble as this little child is the greatest in the Kingdom of Heaven" (Matthew 18:3-4). In Mark's Gospel, Jesus held this child in his arms (see 9:36-37).

The Lord seemed to be saying in this demonstration, "I know all about your impressive titles and degrees. I know about your money and investments, your big-time reputations, and your expensive robes. I know how you scrambled to the top of the heap and how people bow and scrape and step out of the way when you come walking down the street.

"But let me tell you something: This child is way ahead of you when it comes to significance. Look at him! He came to me willingly without pretense, agenda, or hidden motives. He is content to lean back into my arms and trust me with all his heart. He has found the source of true significance, and nothing he can do the rest of his life will make him more significant than he is by trusting me."

The bottom-line issue of significance in God's eternal kingdom is not *who* you are but *whose* you are. It's not what you have, but who has you. It's not what you have accomplished, but what Jesus has accomplished on your behalf. It's not the praise and admiration of people, but the grace and acceptance of God. It's not what you have acquired in life, but what you have surrendered. Any valid attempt at a life of success, whether it be career or home, must begin by bringing yourself and your family into the arms of Jesus.

Perspectives for Living Significantly

Growing in a life of significance isn't a matter of trying harder but of trusting more. Here are a few final guidelines to help you determine if what you are doing is primarily oriented to success or significance.

Examine your motives. Anyone can try to do good things, think good thoughts, and harbor good attitudes. But the acid test for significance is to examine your root motives. Ask yourself these questions:

- ⊕ Why am I doing what I'm doing in this task, this relationship, or this problem?
- ⊕ Am I clawing my own way to success or seeking significance through my relationship with Christ?
- ⊕ Am I out to glorify God or advance my own cause?
- ⊕ Would God be pleased with my motives?

Listen to the Holy Spirit. If you belong to Christ, you will recognize the Spirit's calm, insistent voice in your heart. It's the quiet voice you hear when you lay your head on the pillow at night and review the activities of the day. It's the voice that lovingly but pointedly probes your motivations and beckons you to obedience. You will sense questions like these:

- ⊕ Do you really need to work sixty hours a week to provide for your family?
- ⊕ Are you seeking leadership in the women's Bible study organization in order to serve or be noticed?
- ⊕ Did you discipline your child to train him or because he made you angry?
- ⊕ Are you genuinely happy about your coworker's success, or is envy eating you up?
- ⊕ Did you make that business decision to benefit the company or to feather your own nest?

Listen intently to the Spirit's voice and respond obediently to his probing. He speaks because he loves you and wants you to turn from success to significance.

Open your life to your friends. You and your spouse need the encouragement and counsel of a few Christian friends, people who know you intimately, love you unconditionally, and won't stand for flimsy excuses. You need people close to you who fill Paul's description of a Christian brother or sister:

> Dear brothers and sisters, if another Christian is overcome by some sin, you who are godly should gently and humbly help that person back onto the right path. And be careful not to fall into the same temptation yourself. Share each other's troubles and problems, and in this way obey the law of Christ. If you think you are too important to help someone in need, you are only fooling yourself. You are really a nobody.
>
> Be sure to do what you should, for then you will enjoy the personal satisfaction of having done your work well, and you won't need to compare yourself to anyone else. For we are each responsible for our own conduct. (Galatians 6:1-5)

One way to be responsible for your own conduct is to invite trusted friends to hold you accountable for your motives and actions. Give them permission to get in your face whenever they see you putting success and achievement ahead of the significance of serving Christ.

Strive for excellence, not perfection. Excellence means doing the best you can in God's strength with the time and resources available. Perfection leaves no room for error; perfection says, "Do it right every time, or you fail." The downside of perfectionism isn't pretty. We lose our tolerance for the mistakes and imperfections of others. We make unrealistic demands of our spouses, children, pastor, neighbors, coworkers, and fellow church members.

We need the perspective of the apostle Paul, who before meeting Christ was a successful perfectionist. After reciting his lofty religious pedigree to the Philippian Christians, Paul concluded: "I once thought all these things were so very important, but now I consider them worthless because of what Christ has done. Yes, everything else is worthless when compared with the priceless gain of knowing Christ Jesus my Lord. I have discarded everything else, counting it all as garbage, so that I may have Christ and become one with him. I no longer count on my own goodness or my ability to obey God's law, but I trust Christ to save me. For God's way of making us right with himself depends on faith" (Philippians 3:7-9).

Barb and I pray that you will be successful in all your noble and praiseworthy endeavors. But we trust that you will subject these pursuits to the lordship of Christ and to the nurturing of your spouse and children. With significance as your goal, the success you attain will taste all the sweeter.

Chapter Eight

THE POISON OF
PASSIVITY AND CONTROL

THE FOLLOWING "DARTS" MAY NOT KILL A MARRIAGE, BUT THE poison they inject certainly can bring pain and problems. Have you noticed any of these damaging attitudes among your family members or friends? Have any of these darts hit home in your own marriage?

- ⊕ "It doesn't matter to me. You make the decision. I don't want to think about it."
- ⊕ "Hey, I bring in the money. It's your job to raise the kids."
- ⊕ "Hey, I raise the kids. It's your job to bring in the money."
- ⊕ "If you want more romance and sex in our marriage, you have to initiate it."
- ⊕ "I don't want to talk now. My favorite show is on."
- ⊕ "I worked hard today. You go on to Katy's school program without me."
- ⊕ "Family devotions was your idea, so you get to do it."
- ⊕ "I don't care."

Or perhaps you are more familiar with attitudes at the opposite pole, attitudes that tend to strangle and suffocate a marriage relationship.

- ⊕ "I'll give you more money when I think you need more money."
- ⊕ "We are going to my parents' for Christmas—period."
- ⊕ *"I* make the decisions in this family."
- ⊕ "It's your job to meet my needs."
- ⊕ "I earn the money, so I decide where it goes."
- ⊕ "I know what's best for the kids. We'll raise them my way."
- ⊕ "If you don't get a better job, I'm leaving."
- ⊕ "Do what I want, or there will be no romance tonight."

The two attitudes represented by these lists of statements are among the most harmful threats to your marriage. The first is *passivity,* where one or both partners are lethargic in the relationship, tending not to take an active role at some point or in some areas. The passive spouse communicates through disinterest and inactivity, "That's not my job" or "I don't want to be involved."

The attitude represented by the second list is *control*—the other end of the spectrum from passivity. The controlling spouse is not only involved; he or she tends to dominate to the point of excluding or devaluing his or her partner's involvement or contribution.

Do you see yourself drifting toward or camped at one of these two hurtful poles? Are you a passive, uninvolved spouse or parent? Do you control or dominate your family relationships? If you fail to guard your heart against these attitudes, your marriage and family will suffer.

Barb and I will discuss these threats separately. Since the poison of passivity seems to be more prevalent in men than women, I will address that issue. Then Barb will talk to you about the chokehold of control, where women may have a slight edge over men.

THE I-COULDN'T-CARE-LESS SYNDROME

What has happened to some of the people in our culture today—especially men? When did they become so passive? Why are they content to watch so much of the action instead of participating in it? Having talked with hundreds of couples over the years, Barb and I know that a husband's passivity is one of a wife's most profound pains. He's there, but he's *not* there. He's three feet away, but his mind and heart are light-years out in space. The lights are on, but no one is home.

Being a man, I know how susceptible men are to passivity. It's as if we fray so many neurons in our brain during the work day that we have nothing left when we come home. And Barb assures me that women can be just as susceptible to tune out at home, especially after a demanding day. The problem is that we have people waiting for us after our work is done. They want us to relate to them, not retreat. They need us to engage with them, not escape into a newspaper, TV show, hobby, or a nap on the couch. Do you recognize any of these from your family?

- A fuzzy-headed baby who lights up when you walk in the room even though he can't say "Mommy" or "Daddy" yet.
- A frazzled spouse who has shouldered his or her workload alone during the day.
- A nine-year-old who begs, "Will you play catch with me after dinner?" or "Will you watch me while I practice my clarinet?"
- A high-schooler who doesn't beg for your attention as much but loves it when you ask to hear about his or her day or volunteer to help with homework.

⊕ An adult daughter or son who would walk barefoot across the country just to hear you say, "I'm so proud of you. You're doing a great job. Keep it up."

Why do so many of us forget how to break out of our lethargy and get involved with our spouses and children? Why does a man who promised before God, family, and friends at the wedding to take the steering wheel in his family end up snoozing in the backseat as the years go by? Why does a wife decline the opportunity to be involved in her husband's interests or her kids' outside activities?

I want to talk about passivity and how to guard against it. I will direct my comments primarily to men since such a large number of the women Barb and I counsel tell us their husband's passivity is a major source of pain and fear for them. But we are aware that some of you women may also need to guard against the temptation to passivity as wives and mothers.

Why Spouses Become Passive at Home

Several factors may contribute to your tendency to take a passive role in the home:

1. You may be passive in reaction to your spouse, who is controlling. If your spouse tends to dominate the relationship for some reason, you may have taken a passive role to avoid conflict.

2. You may be passive because that's what your spouse expects. A passive spouse may be the only kind your spouse knows. For example, perhaps your wife grew up in a home where her father was absent, distant, or passive. Her mother had to take the lead to keep the rudderless ship from drifting into the rocks. So your wife takes a controlling role because she believes that you, like her father, won't step up to the plate.

3. You may be passive because that's what you learned growing up.

Your father may have been passive because your mother was dominating. He was your role model, and you accepted that role. Your mother may have grown up in a home where her father overpowered others in the family, and she reacted to it by taking a controlling role. From her perspective, it was "control or be controlled." Your father may have let her rule to keep peace in the family.

4. *You may be passive because you are a short-distance runner.* You read a book, hear a sermon, or attend a conference and realize you need to make a fresh commitment of energy and focus to your family. So you decide to make some changes. You may go to a counselor once or twice, make new strides of involvement with your spouse, engage your kids in activities they always wanted you to do with them, or launch a new family improvement campaign. But then, when you don't see dramatic results in a week, you tend to give up and slip back into your passive role.

5. *You may be passive because you are wounded inside.* Maybe you have been hurt in the past, and as a result of those hurts, you may find it hard to trust. You may tend to protect yourself, pulling away from intimacy in your relationships. It may be an unwitting attempt at getting back at those who hurt you. It may work to a point, but it also kills the hearts of those desiring a relationship with you.

6. *You may be passive because you are just plain lazy.* If you are honest, you might have to admit that you are unmotivated, selfish, and unwilling to take responsibility for being involved with your family. Indifference and laziness can erode a marriage faster than anything else. In some ways, it's easier for a wife to deal with an argument than to deal with a husband who withdraws into silent, preoccupied passivity. She can only wonder,

What happened? He had so much hope and vision. He wanted to make a difference. And I believed in him. But I just don't know anymore.

7. *You may be passive because you confuse leadership with control.* You may have pulled into a shell because you tried leadership and involvement at home, and it didn't work. The problem is, your idea of leadership was laying down the law and barking orders. In other words, you became controlling, and it turned your family off. So you gave up.

No matter what the reason, a hesitance to take leadership or become actively involved at home creates a relational distance that will discourage your spouse and children.

Antidote for Passivity

Do you recognize some tendencies of passivity in your life? If so, you are not condemned to continue in that mode. Here are a few ways to guard your heart against passivity and take a more active role in your relationships at home:

1. *Men, recognize God's design for your role in the family.* The biblical mandate for men is clear. We are called to be the leaders in the home. You may not want this role and responsibility, or you may not feel that you're very good at it. But it is God's design for our lives as husbands and fathers. The apostle Paul spells it out like this:

> For a husband is the head of his wife as Christ is the head of his body, the church; he gave his life to be her Savior. As the church submits to Christ, so you wives must submit to your husbands in everything.
>
> And you husbands must love your wives with the same love Christ showed the church. He gave up his life for her to make her holy and clean, washed by baptism and God's word. He did this to present her to himself as

a glorious church without a spot or wrinkle or any other blemish. Instead, she will be holy and without fault. In the same way, husbands ought to love their wives as they love their own bodies. For a man is actually loving himself when he loves his wife. No one hates his own body but lovingly cares for it, just as Christ cares for his body, which is the church. And we are his body. (Ephesians 5:23-30)

What does it mean to be the head of your wife? Does it mean to control her? Does it mean to dominate and "put your wife in her place"? Absolutely not. Headship is not about domination or power. Headship is about responsibility and being a role model to our families. Genuine leadership involves mentoring those around us—and our wives and children must be at the top of the list. It's not just a matter of telling them what to do; it's a matter of showing them by our example. We can't expect our wives and children to rise above our level as followers of Christ. That's why it is imperative that we become all that God calls us to be. In many ways we are discipling our families through the grace of God that we have experienced firsthand in order to pass it on to them.

We are responsible to lead our homes by serving our wives, just as Christ serves the church. Jesus doesn't beat the church into submission. He doesn't threaten us or bully us or try to intimidate us. No, he continually loves and serves us to the point of giving up his life for us. He is our example of headship in our marriages.

Our wives have a role too: to respect and submit to their husbands (see Ephesians 5:22-24). But we men must set the pace. It is our attitude, behavior, and belief about headship that sets the pace for how our wives relate to us. Be active in your

God-given role of service to your family. When you see a need, meet it. When your wife is hurting, be quick to open your heart to her, offer a word of comfort or encouragement, or just supply a listening ear. It will free your wife to fulfill her role of submission. Your initiation is music to your wife's ears.

2. *If passivity is an issue in your life, confess it and move in another direction.* Repent is a biblical term we don't hear much anymore. It means to change your mind, to stop going in one direction, turn around, and start going in another direction. It's what needs to happen if you as a husband or wife have poisoned your family by being disinterested or uninvolved in some way.

Repentance starts with confession. Psalm 32:5 says, "Finally, I confessed all my sins to you and stopped trying to hide them. I said to myself, 'I will confess my rebellion to the Lord.' And you forgave me! All my guilt is gone." Admit to God that your passive attitude is a sin, and ask for his forgiveness. Next, go to your spouse to confess your shortcoming and ask his or her forgiveness. Then change your direction and assume your God-given responsibility in your family. Your confession won't mean anything if you don't repent by stopping your wrong behavior and heading in a new direction.

3. *Count the hours you spend with your spouse and kids.* My friend Jerry Wunder has three daughters. Several years ago he did something to combat passivity in his relationship with them. Realizing how quickly his girls were growing up, Jerry sat down and computed the number of days he had left with each of them before they left home for college. He then calculated how much more time he could spend with them if he went home from work one hour earlier each day. After completing his calculations, he went to his calendar and boldly slashed out the last hour of each business day so he could go home early.

When Jerry told me about this approach, I sensed the Holy

Spirit's conviction. The next Monday I met with my office staff and made the same adjustment to go home an hour early every day. Yes, we took a financial hit as a result of that decision. But it wasn't as big a hit as my family was taking in my absence. As I moved closer to my family, they in turn moved closer to me. Besides, it made me a hero! Barb loved it, and my daughters got to see more of their dad.

You may not be in a position to shave an hour off your workday even if you wanted to. But perhaps you can reduce some of your other commitments—church, the softball team, community activities, hobbies—to devote more time to being actively involved in the lives of your spouse and kids.

Barb and I have discovered that many people slip into passive mode because their spouses, for some of the reasons listed earlier in this chapter, have taken control in the relationship or family. Men are certainly guilty of trying to dominate their wives and children. The unpleasant extreme is called abuse— physical, sexual, emotional. But often it is the wife and mother who becomes controlling, sometimes by default because her husband is so passive. No matter who is the culprit, a controller can choke the life out of a relationship. Barb will coach you not only on how to identify the tendency to control but also on how to guard your heart and home against it.

THE MY-WAY-OR-THE-HIGHWAY SYNDROME

Most of us have laughed at the line, "If Mama ain't happy, ain't *nobody* happy." But Gary and I know from dealing with couples that it is funny only to a point. When it isn't spoken as a joke, it pictures a controlling person who is making life miserable for others when she—or he—isn't in the driver's seat.

Control can take many different forms in a family relation-

ship. It may be exerted through persuasion, manipulation, pro-
jection of guilt, expression of shame, or through the silent
treatment of withdrawal. Some people grew up in homes where
control was how things got done. You may have had a dad who
controlled you by his disapproval, a mom who controlled you
through guilt, a big brother who controlled you by sitting on
you until you yielded, or a sister who controlled you with a
sharp tongue. A grandfather may have gotten what he wanted
from you through criticism. An aunt may have controlled by
shaming or an uncle by belittling.

Control in a family relationship squashes the human spirit
and stifles loving relationships. You probably know the pain
firsthand. But are you also a controller to some degree? Are
your spouse and children hurting because you tend to ride
roughshod over them? If so, it's time to find out where it's coming from and deal with it, because if you don't, "ain't *nobody*
happy" in your home.

The Four Faces of Control

Gary and I believe there are four reasons why people try to exert
control in relationships. You may be battling control issues in
your life because you have carried one or more of the following
wounds into your marriage and family:

1. Fear. You may have grown up in a home where you were
controlled through intimidation and fear. You were afraid you
wouldn't measure up to Mom's standards. You feared Dad's
rage if you didn't do what he wanted. You cowered in fear that if
you didn't toe the line—whatever line it happened to be—you
wouldn't be safe. You feared the hurt or humiliation. And like
all fear, it wounded your soul.

Deep-seated fear that isn't dealt with will often manifest itself in controlling behaviors. I don't mean that you become an

abusive person in a criminal sense. But your spouse and/or children know that things will get uncomfortable, if not unpleasant, for them if they cross you. This can mean anything from giving them the silent treatment to a blistering reprimand.

If you find that fear is seeping out from under the door of some inner closet in your life, leading you to act in a controlling manner, then meet that fear with a powerful word from God. He instructs us to replace fear with another powerful motivator: love. "Love has no fear because perfect love expels all fear. If we are afraid, it is for fear of judgment, and this shows that his love has not been perfected in us. We love each other as a result of his loving us first" (1 John 4:18-19). Invite God to flood your life with his love and wash away your fear.

2. Insecurity. Controlling behavior can also spring from deep insecurity. Sometimes we control others because we feel it's the only way to deal with our own insecurity. A woman who exhibits this kind of insecurity may never feel safe, even in her own home. As a child, she may have been smothered by the control of a parent, so she may dominate others in order to feel safe. By allowing her husband to take leadership or giving her kids some responsibility, this wife and mother risks losing the control she thinks she needs in order to survive. Allowing others to grow, experience life, make decisions, and expand their own boundaries is a threat to her. So she tends to dominate in order to squelch these threats.

If you are deeply insecure, it's as if your heart has sprung a leak. No matter how much love, attention, and affirmation you receive, it quickly drains away, and you need more. So you continue to make demands on others to fill the emptiness inside. The need is never fully satisfied, so the cycle continues: you demand, your family tries to comply, you are not satisfied, the pain is extended for everyone. The only way to stop the cycle is to submit to divine "heart surgery." Invite God to heal the wounds in your heart and meet your deep need for security.

3. Active and passive aggression. You may be into controlling your family because you can't control yourself, especially your anger. You are the explosive type. When someone doesn't perform to your standards, you blow up—flushed face, loud voice, biting comments. You throw up your hands, you bark and howl, you make threats. Active aggression is control being exercised in the most demanding ways. It frightens others, leads them to feel threatened, and destabilizes homes.

Aggression also has a passive expression that is just as controlling. Instead of a noisy explosion, you may exert your demands through a sullen mood, withdrawal, avoidance, or cold silence. When things at home are going the way you want and people are jumping to your tune, you are warm and agreeable. But when you are not happy, you back off and shut down, punishing everyone with passivity until they toe the line.

In reality, your outbursts are a response to your own hurt that wounds others and leaves you vulnerable for more pain. Proverbs 25:28 states, "A person without self-control is as defenseless as a city with broken-down walls." You need to invite the Holy Spirit's intervention in order to rein in your aggression: "But when the Holy Spirit controls our lives, he will produce this kind of fruit in us: . . . self-control" (Galatians 5:22-23).

4. Low self-esteem. Combining fear with deep insecurity and aggression often results in low self-esteem—how you see yourself and how you think others, including God, see you. You may long to be understood, loved, and accepted at home. If you perceive yourself as unworthy of these qualities, your poor self-esteem may prompt you to act out in a controlling manner.

True self-esteem is established when you are connected in loving relationships that last. Your primary source of healthy self-esteem is God, who loves you unconditionally. Fill your heart and mind with the truth about who you are in Christ, and your self-esteem will grow.

Destructive Criticism

One of the most disheartening and debilitating expressions of controlling behavior is criticism. All of us are prone to complain at home once in a while. But when complaining about circumstances turns into a degrading personal attack on a family member, the wounds delivered are deep and painful.

Complaint becomes criticism when we focus on pointing out what is wrong with a spouse or child. For example:

- ⊕ "The house always looks like a pigsty, and you never lift a finger to help."
- ⊕ "I wish you were half the man my father was."
- ⊕ "The only thing you know how to do well is spend my hard-earned money."
- ⊕ "You are a lazy, irresponsible child. You will never amount to anything."

Criticism doesn't have to be verbal to pierce the heart. Josh and Elaine were having dinner out with friends. Josh mentioned to Bob that he had just signed up for a new credit card, something he had failed to tell his wife. Elaine said nothing, but the laser beams of disapproval and criticism in her hot glare cut deep into Josh's heart. Sometimes you can wound with a look, the shrug of a shoulder, or arms crossed in defiance.

Hurtful criticism isn't always directed at your spouse or child. It may be voiced to someone else. When Kathleen is with her girlfriends, she can't resist dragging out all the dirty laundry from home. It mostly comes out in criticism of her husband. She wants her friends to feel sorry for her, which is a subtle act of control. Eventually indirect criticism will get back to the principal target, and the wound will be even greater.

Sometimes a critical, controlling spirit may be expressed in what you *don't* say or do. The stark absence of encouragement and affirmation can be just as damaging as cutting words of criticism. For Amy, it's not what she says that hurts Jake; it's what she doesn't say. Jake can't remember the last time she complimented him or thanked him for anything. What's worse, Amy is quick to speak a positive word to other men they know: their minister, her father, even her doctor. The lack of positive feedback can be just as hurtful as a verbal barrage of criticism.

Another expression of criticism intended to control a spouse or child is comparison. Mike knew Frieda wanted a big house, the bigger the better. And he worked hard to get it for her. But instead of saying, "Thank you" or "I'm so proud of how you worked for this," Frieda starts a new list based on the things her friends' husbands have given their wives. Comparison is a backdoor way of saying, "You're not good enough" or "You didn't do what I expected."

Do you tend to control or badger your spouse or children through criticism? Do you want to break the critical cycle? Here are a few guidelines:

Complain but don't blame. There may be times when you will complain about a problem at home, but don't use that situation as an excuse to find fault with your spouse or child. The idea is to fix the problem, not affix blame. Take the initiative to make things right without damaging your relationships with blame.

Use "I" statements instead of "you" statements. Instead of criticizing by saying, "You always embarrass me in front of our friends," say, "I feel hurt when you talk about my weight with our friends." When you start by pointing the finger of blame, you are forgetting the importance of examining your own heart. Pray along with David, "Search me, O God, and know my heart; test me and know my thoughts. Point out anything in me that offends you, and lead me along the path of everlasting life" (Psalm 139:23-24). When you use "I" statements, you invite your spouse to respond to your pain instead of defend himself or herself from your attack.

Be factual. Instead of blasting your spouse or child over a messy kitchen, be specific without attacking. Try something like, "I get frustrated when you forget to put caps on bottles and leave dishes in the sink. It would help if you remember to tighten those lids and put your plates in the dishwasher."

Take care of issues quickly. Don't fall into the pattern of letting hurts build up and then exploding with criticism. Ephesians 4:26 says, "Don't let the sun go down while you are still angry." The sooner you take care of conflicts, the less chance you will drift into a critical spirit.

How are you exerting hurtful control in your family? Is it by pulling out of involvement with your spouse? Are you punishing your spouse by neglecting to meet a genuine need or by being harsh and dominant with your children? Does your family sense that you are a my-way-or-the-highway kind of person? Instead of yielding to the temptation to control and manipulate your family, you need to surrender your controlling tendencies to Christ. It's ironic: You will gain better control of your life and how you treat others when you yield control to him. You can trust Christ to move a loved one's heart or change his or her behavior. You can tell everything to him instead of getting in a family member's face and assuming control.

Those who rely on well-practiced controlling techniques to get their own way and satisfy their needs are living without the power of the Holy Spirit. When you try to scheme, coerce, manipulate, or connive your way through life, the result will be short-term gain at best and eternal loss at worst. You may get what you want initially, but you will not get peace or happiness in the bargain. Jesus said, "If you cling to your life, you will lose it; but if you give it up for me, you will find it" (Matthew 10:39). Give God control and live.

Part Three

THE DEFENSE OF YOUR MARRIAGE

Chapter Nine

A MARRIAGE ON THE ROCKS

Your hearts and the marriage you have entered into together are under attack. We live in a culture that condones and even promotes sex and cohabitation before marriage, marriages of convenience, and quickie divorces. Lifetime commitment in marriage and marital fidelity are often seen as prudish, outdated, and boring. And since divorce-proof marriages are God's design, Satan is active and relentless in his attempt to disrupt them, spoil them, or destroy them. You may think of your marriage as a romantic castle of love, but hardly a day goes by when the walls around you are not under siege in some way.

In the previous two parts of this book, Barb and I have alerted you to the reality of this assault and described a number of specific threats to a godly marriage. Along the way, we have coached you on some practical, biblical skills for guarding your hearts and your home against these sinister threats. Now it's time to bring out the big guns. In this section we want to equip you for the all-out defense of your marriage. These are the rock-solid, foundational basics of what we call *guarding love*. Without this foundation, your castle is on shaky ground. This final section of the book will help you strengthen the foundation of your marriage.

You may say, "Hey, we've been married for some years now. It's a little late to be working on the foundation." Not really. When you build a house, you definitely want to pour the foundation before you go ahead with the framing, plumbing, electrical, drywall, and paint. But few of us started our marriages with that kind of forethought. Be honest now: Were you thoroughly prepared for marriage before you walked down the aisle and said, "I do"? Did you understand all of the complex things that happen when two people become one? Were you emotionally, mentally, and spiritually ready to give yourself 100 percent to another person?

Barb and I have yet to meet someone who can answer those questions with an unequivocal "Yes!" Rather, we hear couples say something like, "We were in love, so we got married. We really didn't know each other very well, and we didn't have much of an idea what we were getting ourselves into." That's why we have to keep working on the foundation. You can be— and should be—continually fortifying your foundation, even as you move on with day-to-day married life. The stronger the foundation, the greater your defense against the assault on your marriage.

In this chapter we begin with the cornerstone.

GET THE PEACE OF THE ROCK

Barb and I have a "rock collection" that forms the cornerstone of our marriage. There are three rocks in our collection. The first rock was big enough to cover the opening of the most famous tomb in history, but it didn't stay there. The second rock is small enough to hold in my hand, and that's where it was on the most important day of my life. The third rock is broad enough and strong enough to support our marriage and yours. We want to tell you about each of them.

The Rock That Wouldn't Stay Put

This rock is the one the Roman soldiers rolled in front of the tomb to lock away the lifeless body of Jesus Christ. It's the most important rock in the Bible. Pontius Pilate, the Roman governor, assumed that a huge boulder, an official seal, and a contingent of Roman guards would keep Jesus from rising from the grave. But it didn't work. An angel rolled away the stone so the world could see that Jesus is alive, ready to give eternal life to all who believe.

Our marriage is built on the foundation of Christ's death, burial, and triumphant resurrection. The Resurrection is the pivotal event in human history, the key to the Christian life, the hope of every believer. As the apostle Paul said, "If Christ has not been raised, then your faith is useless, and you are still under condemnation for your sins. . . . And if we have hope in Christ only for this life, we are the most miserable people in the world" (1 Corinthians 15:17-19). Barb and I would have no hope for our lives, let alone our marriage, apart from Christ's triumph over the grave. If we had no hope for a future in heaven with Christ after this life is over, we may as well "eat, drink, and be merry." What's the point of living for significance? And what's the point of marital fidelity?

But because Christ is alive, we *do* have a hope that extends throughout life and into eternity. As a result, our lives and our marriage have a meaning that is spiritual as well as physical and emotional. The rock that rolled away from the tomb opened the way for our lives individually and as a couple.

Is Christ's "tomb stone" part of the foundation for your marriage? Do you and your spouse accept that the death and resurrection of Jesus Christ is God's only provision for your sin and your hope for the future? If not, Barb and I urge you to welcome this truth into your relationship and open your hearts to a personal relationship with the living Christ.

The Rock of Our Salvation

We have a second rock that has tremendous meaning in both of our lives, but especially mine. Many years ago I held on to this rock for dear life in the midst of a ferocious battle over my very soul. This little rock represents the day many years ago when my life was transformed by Jesus Christ. My personal relationship with the resurrected Christ—as well as Barb's—is foundational to the health of our marriage.

But since Barb met Christ several months before I did, I want her to tell her story first.

At the age of nineteen, I was on a search for God and didn't even know it. I was a sophomore at Drake University in my home town of Des Moines, going for all the fun college life was supposed to deliver. But all the parties and friends didn't satisfy me. I knew there had to be more to life, but I had no idea what it was.

Like so many people, I was raised in a good home with loving parents. And like most people in my neighborhood, we went to church every Sunday. But to me, religion was traditional and formal. I had no understanding that a person's life could be transformed through a living, breathing relationship with Jesus Christ. The concept never entered my mind. I had been taught about the love of Jesus since I was a little girl. A picture of Christ even occupied an honored place on the wall in our home. I knew that he died and rose again, and I accepted the fact that he was holy and I was not. But these were just religious facts, all head knowledge with very little heart experience.

For many years my mother belonged to a weekly prayer group that met in our home, and I often saw her go to her knees in prayer. She told me that her group was praying for me, and since I struggled all through school, I needed those prayers. But I had no idea God wanted to be more involved in my life than just my studies. When my older brother came home for Christmas break in 1972, God made his presence and power known to me in a dramatic, life-changing way.

I arrived home from a party one night to find that the picture of Jesus was missing from the wall. I was mortified; nobody ever touched that picture. Coming into my brother's room, I found the picture propped up in a chair. Barry was gazing at it as if someone was sitting in the chair, visiting with him. "Barry," I said in a scolding tone, hands on hips, "I don't know what kind of games you're into, but you get that picture of Christ back on the wall."

"Barbie, you'd better sit down," he said, smiling. "I have something wonderful to tell you." Normally Barry avoided me and rarely wanted to talk to me. But this Christmas break he had been different. He had been treating me nicely for a change. So I sat down.

My brother proceeded to tell me that he had given his life to Jesus Christ. Then he pulled out a little booklet and shared with me the Four Spiritual Laws from Campus Crusade for Christ. I was blown away. It had never occurred to me that Jesus had died for me personally. I never realized I could have a personal relationship with Christ.

When Barry said, "Barbie, God loves you and has a wonderful plan for your life," I knew I had found the missing piece of the puzzle I had been looking for all my life. For the first time the gospel made perfect sense. So on December 17, 1972, at 10:45 P.M., I sat beside my brother as he led me in a prayer inviting Jesus Christ into my life. My relationship with Christ, which began that night, has been the foundation stone for my life.

From that night on I became a praying woman. I began talking to Jesus as I would talk to my best friend. One of the first things I prayed for was a man who loved God as much as I did. I also prayed for my grades to improve in college. To my mom's surprise, I made the honor roll at Drake within a year. As for the other prayer, God was already at work behind the scenes.

At Barry's encouragement, I got involved with the local chapter of Campus Crusade for Christ so that I could be discipled. About the same time, I began dating a handsome, gregarious student. He would meet with me and others involved in Campus Crusade to question and debate Christianity. I knew Gary wasn't a Christian, but I kept praying for him, and I could tell God was working in his heart. I'll let him tell the rest of the story.

Barb and I had been dating for about six months when she invited me over to her parents' house one evening for dinner. As the evening progressed, something came over me, a compulsion to be alone. In reality, it was an invitation from God to come into his presence. His outstretched hand beckoned me that night. I answered and my life story was altered for eternity.

For several months prior to that evening, Barb and a few other Christian students at Drake had been trying to explain something brand-new to me: that I could have a personal relationship with Jesus Christ. I grew up in a family that respected God and went to church, but no one ever explained to me the possibility of enjoying a personal relationship with Christ. It sounded so good, but my pride got in the way. I took a skeptic's approach and set out to disprove the truth of the resurrection of Christ.

I tore into the Scriptures, met with Christians, and tried a local church where the gospel was taught. I asked question after question of anyone who would listen. A man named Gordon

Mooney from Campus Crusade for Christ was instrumental in helping me sort through this new information. I listened to Barbara discuss her newfound faith in Christ, and I was torn apart. On one hand, I wanted nothing more than to believe that Jesus Christ died for me and my sins. On the other hand, my pride was so strong that I found myself running from the truth, fearing the changes God would make in my life. Yet deep in my heart I knew I needed to yield to him.

So on that summer evening in 1973, after a dinner of chicken and dumplings with Barb and her parents, the turmoil inside me came to a head. I stood up to excuse myself, which confused Barb because she thought we were going out together. I said, "Barb, I just need to be alone for a while. I'm going to take a walk." Then I headed out the door.

Several minutes later I found myself at a construction site, standing next to a pile of rocks that was destined to become part of a concrete parking lot. I climbed up on that pile of rocks and sat down, just me and God. For the next hour, the two of us battled over who would lay claim to my soul. At one point I grabbed a small rock off that pile, squeezed it with all my might, and began to pray. "God, I don't know why you want a person like me. I have disappointed you, my parents, Barb, and myself. I blow it every time I turn around. But the more I learn about you, the more I know that I need you in my life."

As I drew closer to God that night, another power joined the battle trying to pull me away. "Why would God want you, Gary?" I heard the enemy say. "You have already screwed up your life. You aren't worth saving. God only wants the best, and you are nothing but a loser." Every loving word from God was countered by an attack from Satan. And every foul accusation was followed by God's promise of forgiveness and acceptance.

As the battle raged, I gripped that little rock in my hand. I told both God and Satan that if I became a Christian that night, I would keep that rock for the rest of my life. But if I decided to reject Christ, I would throw it as far as I could into the night and never seek him again.

Finally, I cried out to God, "I don't know why you want me. But I realize you have a plan for me. I know I have sinned, so I ask you to forgive me and come into my heart right now on this rock pile. God, I want you to be my Savior and my Lord."

As I finished that prayer, it was as if the weight of that entire rock pile was lifted from my shoulders. The war was over, the chains were broken, I was free. I raced to a nearby phone booth and called Barb to meet me on the street. As she approached under the streetlight, before I could say a word, she called out, "You just accepted Jesus Christ!" Her face was beaming like I had never seen it before. Two years later we became husband and wife.

I still have that small rock. I keep it in Barb's jewelry box. It symbolizes something very important to both of us. It represents the day I stepped from death into life, from darkness into light. It was the day I gave control of my life to the One to whom Barb had also yielded control. With Christ as our Savior and Lord, we both look to him to nurture our lives and our marriage. He is the Rock of our salvation and the Rock of our marriage.

The apostle Paul wrote to the Roman Christians, "If you confess with your mouth that Jesus is Lord and believe in your heart that God raised him from the dead, you will be saved" (Romans 10:9). Earlier we challenged you to take the second step in this verse: to believe that Jesus died and was raised for your salvation. Now we urge you to make your belief personal, as Barb and I did, by declaring that Jesus Christ is your Lord. The foundation for your marriage cannot be more solid than when you are both taking orders from the same Lord. A husband's and a wife's personal relationship with Jesus Christ is vital to a healthy, growing marriage.

A Rock That Will Support a Castle

There is another rock in our collection, one that is indispensable to our marriage. It is the rock mentioned in this parable by Jesus: "Anyone who listens to my teaching and obeys me is wise, like a person who builds a house on solid rock. Though the rain comes in torrents and the floodwaters rise and the winds beat against that house, it won't collapse, because it is built on rock. But anyone who hears my teaching and ignores it is foolish, like a person who builds a house on sand. When the rains and floods come and the winds beat against that house, it will fall with a mighty crash" (Matthew 7:24-27).

This element of the foundation for our marriage is our obedience to the Lord Jesus Christ. Following God's plan for marriage, as found in his Word, is what makes our life together work. For example, God's Word instructs, "You husbands must love your wives with the same love Christ showed the church" (Ephesians 5:25). When I love Barb selflessly and sacrificially as Christ loved us, our marriage grows stronger. When I get selfish and possessive, our relationship suffers. It's the same with all of God's instructions for the marriage relationship. When we comply with them, our "house"—the marriage we build on this solid foundation—can withstand all the storms of life. When we disregard God's directives, we are vulnerable to the elements.

A lot of us don't think about this foundation until the storm hits. Then we regret our sloppy workmanship. We must build the castle of our marriages in such a way that, whether we are being pummeled by the storms of life—sick kids, overwhelming bills, marital pain, stress—or everything is going great, the foundation beneath us will remain secure, like a rock. The daily fortification of our marriage foundation equates to daily obedience to God's plan for marriage.

FOUNDATION INSPECTION

Take a long, hard look at the present condition of your marriage's foundation. You need all three elements we have discussed in this chapter: the rock of Christ's resurrection, the rock of your personal commitment to the risen Christ, and the rock of daily obedience to God's Word. You can't pick and choose; it's a package deal. If you want to guard your heart and home against the assault on your marriage and family, you need a complete foundation.

Barb and I encourage you to think carefully about the three questions below. As you do so, if you feel the need to take a step toward solidifying any of these elements of your marriage foundation, we invite you to respond by praying with us.

1. Are you committed to the truth of Christ's death and resurrection? If so, then pray this prayer with us: "Heavenly Father, I acknowledge right now that your Son, Jesus Christ, came to earth in human form, was crucified on the cross for my sins, and was raised from the dead so that I may have new life in him. I admit that my life and my marriage have no hope for true fulfillment and fruitfulness apart from the resurrection power of Christ. I commit myself to the truth that Jesus is alive and ready to infuse my life and my marriage with his power. Amen."

2. Have you invited Jesus Christ into your life as your Savior and Lord? If you would like to do that now, pray with us: "God, I am convinced that I have fallen short of your standards for righteousness and have sinned against you. I confess my sin and am sorry. I ask you to come into my life right now. I receive your Son, Jesus Christ, as my Savior and Lord, and I ask you to forgive my sins. Help me be the kind of person, spouse, and parent you want me to be. Amen."

3. Are you walking in daily obedience to God's Word in your personal life and in your marriage? If you want to make a commitment, pray this prayer with us: "Lord, I believe that 'all Scripture is inspired by God and is useful to teach us what is true and to make us realize what is wrong in our lives. It straightens us out and teaches us to do what is right,' as it says in 2 Timothy 3:16. I have not been fully obedient to your Word, and the difficulties in my personal and family life are evidence of my failure. Help me understand, apply, and obey your Word in all my activities, especially as a spouse and parent. Amen."

A vital relationship with Jesus Christ and his Word must be your number one priority in life. Without Christ as the Rock of your salvation, you will be vulnerable to the enemy's attacks on you and your family. Jesus doesn't promise Christians that there will be no storms in their lives. He doesn't make you impervious to attack. Rather, with Christ as your Lord and his Word as your guide, you have every resource you need to withstand anything life throws at you and even come out stronger.

Barb and I challenge you to acknowledge that serving God individually and as a couple is your most important purpose in life. This is the cornerstone for guarding your heart and home. Nothing is more important. Yet nothing promises such extravagant rewards for you as a spouse and parent.

Chapter Ten

GUARD YOUR OWN HEART

Davids CALLED IN TO OUR DAILY RADIO PROGRAM A FEW months ago. His voice was strong and determined as he spoke. "Gary and Barb," he began, "I have listened to you almost every day for over a year. I have heard men and women call in to share their hearts and their hurts with you, to be encouraged by you, and to get your coaching tips for their marriages. I'm convinced that you have given counsel not only from your hearts but from the heart of God. It has been such an encouragement to me."

"Thanks, David," I said. "Now what can we do for you?"

"I want in my own life what you two are experiencing: not a perfect marriage, but one that is rich with honesty and integrity, a marriage that is making a difference in the lives of husband and wife."

"We want that kind of marriage for you too, David," Barb inserted.

"Well, I have a problem. I have kept something from my wife for over ten years. I had an affair, but I never told her about it. I never told anyone until recently when I shared my secret with my accountability partner. As I confessed to him, he listened without judging. He took me to Scripture and prayed with me. It's kind of like you guys talk about on the radio. He was 'God with skin on' for me."

"That's great, David," I said. "What happened next?"

"After about two hours, with our eyes still wet with tears, he asked me a tough question: 'What are you going to do about telling your wife?' I guess I knew it was coming. I felt both relieved and scared. But then the doubts began racing through my head: *What if I do tell Joanne and she walks away? Am I being selfish wanting to come clean with her, or could this be the beginning of a new level of commitment in our marriage?*

"Then I thought of how you two have coached people through their fears and conflicts and given them a road map to restoration. That's why I'm calling today. I want what you describe as a godly marriage, one with emotional, spiritual, and sexual intimacy that is clean and rich with integrity. How do I get there after what I have done?"

Barb and I glanced at each other. We both sensed that healing was about to begin for this young man. Then we began to coach him. I said, "Your first step toward the marriage you want is to confess your unfaithfulness to your wife. As long as you hide this secret from her, you will never experience the blessing waiting for you on the other side of your pain."

"And if you don't own up to your sin, David," Barb added, "you will live with that pain every day. You will feel guilty whenever you connect with your wife emotionally. When you try to connect with her spiritually, you will feel the conviction of the Holy Spirit rise up within you. And when you connect with her sexually, the shame messages from the enemy will ring in your ears. But when you get it out in the open, the healing can start, and all this pain will eventually go away."

David was silent as he processed our words. Then I added, "David, we encourage you to pray. Ask your buddy to pray for you, and know that we will be praying too. Then approach your wife with humility, obedience, and courage, and seek her forgiveness." We concluded by praying with David on the air, asking God to give him the desire of his heart: a marriage without the deceit and lies that were sabotaging him at every turn.

Barb and I couldn't get David off our minds. On the way home that night we agreed that his marriage was on the brink. What would happen when he confessed his infidelity? Would Joanne reject him and throw him out or forgive him? Would she call a divorce attorney or walk through the restoration process with her husband?

A few weeks went by, then David called again. We often won't take repeat callers on the program, but you couldn't keep us away from that call. "Gary and Barb," David began, "I need to tell you the rest of the story. Two nights ago, after a lot of prayer, I approached Joanne with a broken heart and told her of my affair ten years ago. She was in shock and very angry. We both cried. I asked Joanne to prayerfully consider a 'do-over,' giving me and our marriage a fresh start."

"What did she say?" Barb asked.

"She said not now, not yet. We went to sleep exhausted. But I stared at the ceiling half the night wondering if the morning would bring any relief. What will happen when she wakes up and realizes it wasn't a bad dream? Will she still want me? Can she ever forgive me?"

"That had to be tough," I said.

David continued. "A few hours ago at my office, I received an e-mail from her. It contained just these words: 'Do-over granted.' I sat in my office with tears streaming down my face, thanking God that my marriage could begin to heal. We still have a long way to go, but I know God doesn't want this marriage to end. It is really just the beginning. Do I deserve this wonderful woman and her forgiveness? No way. But I am thankful she loves God enough to believe we can begin again."

Barb and I are so blessed by David's story. And we are encouraged by the truth that God promises do-overs when we blow it. The psalmist writes, "The Lord is merciful and gracious; he is slow to get angry and full of unfailing love. He will not constantly accuse us, nor remain angry forever. He has not punished us for all our sins, nor does he deal with us as we deserve" (Psalm 103:8-10). He is eager to hear our humble confession and forgive our sin: "If my people who are called by my name will humble themselves and pray and seek my face and turn from their wicked ways, I will hear from heaven and will forgive their sins and heal their land" (2 Chronicles 7:14).

No matter how you have sinned against God and your spouse, God stands ready to give you a new start.

God also encourages us to be very generous with do-overs in our relationships, as illustrated in Matthew 18:21-22. Peter asked Jesus how often he should forgive those who sin against him. Then he suggested that forgiving someone seven times might be a generous step. Jesus responded, "No! . . . seventy times seven!" His point was clear: There should be no limit to our forgiveness because there is no limit to God's forgiveness.

No matter how your spouse has hurt you in the past or may hurt you in the future, you have Jesus' encouragement to forgive him or her again and again and again.

SOMETHING BETTER THAN A DO-OVER

As wonderful and as available as forgiveness is to believers, there is something better. It's the peace of never having anything to confess. We're not talking about sinless perfection here because that is unachievable in this life. We will occasionally blow it with God and with our families. But that doesn't mean we are slaves to sin or powerless against temptation. The apostle

John wrote, "The Spirit who lives in you is greater than the spirit who lives in the world" (1 John 4:4).

You can begin each day with a clean slate and live obediently in the power of the Holy Spirit within you. You can say no to the threats to your marriage and to the temptations to be less than the person God called you to be in your home. It begins with the determination to guard your own heart. That's right, you are responsible for your own thoughts, words, and actions. You are the one who must say "No way!" when you are tempted to compromise your role as husband, wife, or parent.

In this chapter we want to coach you on five vital principles for defending your marriage and family by guarding your own heart. Guarding love starts with you. In addition to guarding your own heart, you have the privilege and responsibility to guard your spouse's heart. In chapter 11 Barb will write to wives on how to guard their husbands' hearts. Then in chapter 12 I will coach men on how to guard their wives' hearts.

1. Commit to the Task of Guarding Your Heart
Your marriage is under attack, and your enemy is real. Satan is intent on ripping your family apart. And if he can't push you into an ugly divorce, he will just keep pecking away to make your life as miserable as he can. I hope he never tricks you into sexual sin as he did with David. But he will keep trying to separate you from your spouse and children through pride, fear, anger, lies, self-absorption, self-protection—just to name a few of his weapons. And wherever you fail to guard your own heart, he can gain a foothold.

So you need a battle mentality. You need to draw a line in the sand and declare to the enemy of your heart, "No way, not me. Not now. Not ever." You need to make a commitment to guard your heart at all costs. Then you need to live out that commitment on a daily basis.

Don't you love the resolve of Joseph in the Old Testament? Here's a godly man who fought an uphill battle most of his life. His older brothers sold him to slave traders, but he trusted God. When his master's wife couldn't seduce him, she framed him for sexual assault. But Joseph trusted God. In prison, he did a favor for someone who could get him pardoned, but the guy forgot him. Still, Joseph trusted God. Here was a man with a firm commitment and a well-guarded heart.

Let's go back to the incident with Potiphar's wife in Genesis 39. Apparently Joseph was going about his daily business of tending to his master's home. Mrs. Potiphar threw herself at him, brashly beckoning him into bed with her. Potiphar was gone. She and Joseph were alone in the house. The coast was clear. How did Joseph resist such enticement?

I want you to notice what Joseph said because it is a key for committing to guard your own heart in any compromising circumstance: "How could I ever do such a wicked thing? It would be a great sin against God" (Genesis 39:9). This wasn't some excuse he made up on the spot in order to slip away. He had committed to live in purity and obedience to God long before Mrs. Potiphar came on the scene. When this tempting opportunity presented itself, his solid commitment kicked into gear: "How could I? It's unthinkable. It's wrong. It's a sin, and I won't do it."

You need that same level of commitment to guarding your heart. You need to decide now that you will not knowingly do or say anything that will damage your marriage. Then you have a point of reference for anything Satan may throw at you. When you are tempted to criticize your child, you respond, "That's not what I'm about. It's wrong. I'm not doing it." When you think about shading the truth with your spouse to avoid a conflict, you say, "How could I do something so wrong? I'm committed to living and speaking the truth. So I can't lie." And with every victorious stand against the threats to your marriage, your commitment will grow stronger.

Individually and as a couple, Barb and I have committed ourselves to living obediently and creating a legacy that honors Jesus Christ. We want to leave behind two life stories that will encourage and equip our children and grandchildren for their marriages. We invite you to join us in that commitment. You may want to do something concrete, such as carefully wording your commitment and printing it on paper. Then sign it, and keep it where you will see it often. Create one for yourself, then you and your spouse write your corporate commitment.

Determine to live out that commitment on a daily basis. How? By being consistent with the basics. Study the Bible on a daily basis. Share what you read and discover with your spouse. Pray daily, on your own and with your spouse. Confess to God any known sin in your life so God can use you. Live above reproach in all your activities so that God's light can shine through you and point your family members and others to Christ.

2. Ask the Lord to Protect Your Heart

Having resolved to guard your heart against all threats to your marriage and family, how much of your commitment can you keep in your own power? If your answer was anything but zero, you may need to rethink it. Jesus told us, "I am the vine; you are the branches. Those who remain in me, and I in them, will produce much fruit. For apart from me you can do nothing" (John 15:5). That's right, we can't do anything apart from our dependence on Jesus Christ. If you want to guard your heart, you need to see yourself as a branch that is utterly dependent on the vine to which you are attached.

Jesus is the vine, we are the branches. You need to rely on

him daily to guard your heart. Your pastor can't guard your heart for you, and your favorite TV preacher can't do it. Your Bible study group, your accountability partners, and all the good Christian books and tapes you can get your hands on can't do it either. All of these things can encourage you and teach you, but only Christ can guard your heart. You can't do anything without Jesus, but look what you can do *with* him. The apostle Paul testifies with confidence, "I can do everything with the help of Christ who gives me the strength I need" (Philippians 4:13).

Ask the Lord to protect your heart. Make it your daily prayer. Paraphrase John 15:5 and Philippians 4:13 as you pray: "Lord, apart from you I can do zero. But with your help I can do everything I need to do to guard my heart and my family." Pray this prayer with your spouse, perhaps before your feet even hit the floor in the morning. The tighter your connection to the vine, the better equipped you will be to withstand the daily threats to your life and marriage.

3. Establish Openness with God

God knows our hearts. He knows our fears. He knows our sins. He knows our deepest thoughts before we even think them. And yet how often we try to ignore or gloss over our inner battles, temptations, and attitudes hoping he won't notice. We mistakenly think if we press on with a business-as-usual mindset that he won't be offended.

A vital key to guarding your heart is to come clean with God about what he already knows and sees. He knows about your tempting thoughts, so why not confess them to him when they happen? He hears your sharp retort to your spouse, so why not agree with him on the spot that it was wrong? Let God into your heart. Your thoughts, words, and deeds don't catch him by surprise. He doesn't gasp in horror when you fail to guard your heart in some way. He has promised never to reject you, leave you, or turn his back on you. So you can confidently expose your hurts, your sins, your temptations, your failures, and your very life to him.

Don't pull back from God when you blow it. Be open with him. Tell him everything, including how you feel. He's not going away. He is available to you all day, every day. He wants to be involved in everything you are involved in, including your marriage. As you open yourself to him from the heart, you connect with the lifeblood of the vine, Jesus Christ, the source for guarding your heart.

4. Keep Short Accounts

David, the man we counseled on the radio to confess his long-buried affair, is an example of what can happen when you bury conflicts with your spouse instead of confessing them and forgiving them. David kept a long account of deceit that accrued a ledger full of painful interest. And the enemy loved every minute, hour, week, and year that David lived this lie at home. Think of the years of intimacy wasted as he kept his secret hidden. It was only by the grace of God that his wife Joanne agreed to a do-over in their marriage. David's hidden sin could have resulted in divorce.

It is important to guard your own heart by keeping short accounts with your spouse. Take responsibility for confessing your wrongs immediately, asking forgiveness, and making amends. God wants us to keep short accounts so we can be clean vessels in his service, so he can do his will in our lives, and so he can accomplish his plans for us. When we fail to close the loops of conflicts with our spouses, he can't work through us.

First Peter 3:7 instructs men, "You husbands must give honor to your wives. Treat her with understanding as you live together. She may be weaker than you are, but she is your equal partner in God's gift of new life. If you don't treat her as you should, your prayers will not be heard." When a man says to me, "I just don't feel that God is using me," I ask him two questions. First I ask, "How is your prayer life and your time in God's Word?" Often he will say, "My prayers don't seem to be getting past the ceiling, and my Bible study time is irregular." I'm not surprised. Then I ask, "How are you treating your wife? Is there anything between you that needs to be confessed and forgiven?" And usually there is.

It's a spiritual principle. If you are not keeping short accounts with your spouse, you can't expect God to do much in your life. When I have a conflict with Barb, my prayer life gets all messed up. When I'm holding a grudge at home, it seems like nothing else goes right. When I wrong her and fail to ask forgiveness, I'm off center until I do. And when I clean it up with my bride, I connect with God in a much better way. Whenever something is wrong between you—even when you don't know what it is—take the initiative to clear it up.

5. Be Accountable to Others

If David had not gone to his friend with his secret and if his friend had not loved him in the midst of his pain, David would still be living in the dark. A significant part of guarding your own heart is being accountable to a friend or small group of friends. You need to grant someone access to your thoughts, decisions, and attitudes—not to control you or heap guilt on you, but to pray with you, encourage you, and fight the good fight with you. Your spouse is your number one confidant and friend. But you need someone else, someone of your own sex who can identify with your struggles.

Barb and I are not talking about being an open book with anyone and everyone. We mean finding a few trusted friends who know you well and love you unconditionally. And we're not talking about a "secret society" where you talk about issues you would never talk about with your spouses. We mean a friend or two with whom you share information your spouse has allowed you to share. Do you have someone like this in your life?

The enemy loves to isolate you from relationships with godly friends. He doesn't want you to rely on the strength of others when he has thrown you into the muck. But God loves to lift you out of the muck and clean you up, and he frequently uses godly friends to do it. But you have to open up to them and trust them. A well-guarded heart does not walk through life's challenges alone. You need to find godly men or women who will ask you the tough questions:

⊕ Have you been reading the Bible?
⊕ Is your prayer life consistent?
⊕ What unconfessed sin might be blocking God's work in you?
⊕ What impure thoughts, motives, or attitudes need to be rooted out?

Godly friends help watch our flanks, gently point out our blind spots, and nudge us through periods of confession and restoration. The key here is to never walk alone. The Lord is with us, to be sure. And he puts other helpful people into our lives when we are open to them and allow them in. It starts with God, then your spouse, who is your primary accountability partner, and possibly a small group of men or women who are willing to walk with you. You shouldn't walk alone, and you don't need to walk alone. Ask God to bring people into your life who will help you guard your heart.

In the next chapter Barb is going to share with you women seven keys to guarding your husband's heart. Men, we will have our turn in chapter 12. However, Barb and I suggest that you read the chapter addressed to your spouse as well as the one geared for you. Use these chapters to foster meaningful communication between you about guarding each other's heart.

Chapter Eleven

GUARD YOUR HUSBAND'S HEART

A HUSBAND AND WIFE NEED TO FORGE A DEEP INTERDEPEN-
dence through relying on each other. We need to come to the
place where we can say to our spouse, "I will depend on you to
guard and protect my heart and my life, to fight beside me always." Most couples develop this deep mutual bond over a period of years and through the trials of their life together. That's
certainly how it happened with Gary and me.

It was April of 1983, and I was struggling as a young wife.
Gary was in the thick of his work and doctoral studies, leaving
me with all of the responsibility to care for our girls and take
care of an older home. My plate was full from all the duties of
mothering and maintaining family life virtually alone. Our lifestyle was so focused on getting Gary through school that I was
burning out. At times I felt Gary, Sarah, and Missy needed more
from me than I had to give.

One day as I was vacuuming, I thought, *Why am I doing all the
work in this marriage? Why try? Things are never going to change.* I had
kept myself going through those years by listening to good biblical teaching on Christian radio. But I was growing weary.
Things weren't turning out the way I wanted. So in the silence
of my heart that day, a switch was flipped. I thought, *That's it. I
quit, I'm done. I'm not trying anymore.*

Deep down inside, I had allowed my love for Gary and my

longing for the ideal family to skew my priorities. I had taken the responsibility for what I thought our marriage should be. I had taken my eyes off God and put them on my husband. I viewed Gary as my "home-improvement project." And since he wasn't conforming to my ideal, I gave up—not because I got smart, but because I was tired. I didn't think all the good I was doing was making a difference. I was convinced that our discouraging lifestyle was never going to change. In reality, I was contributing a big share by allowing my heart to harden toward Gary through self-pity and pride.

Maybe you have also grown weary in your marriage and parenting. You have tried everything you know to do, but your situation hasn't changed. Your husband doesn't seem to appreciate what you do for him. Your kids always need something from you. You feel hopeless and discouraged with no change in sight. Like me, you may have given up.

Let me encourage you. God is working in your situation, even though you may not see it right now. Remember when Elisha and his servant were in the city of Dothan surrounded by the enemy army? The servant was terrified, but Elisha was calm. He prayed, "O Lord, open his eyes and let him see!" (2 Kings 6:17). At that moment God opened the servant's eyes to see that the enemy was surrounded by horses and chariots of fire. God was there all along; the servant just didn't see him.

I pray that God will also open your eyes to see that God is already at work in your marriage. He was at work in my marriage even when I gave up. I finally glimpsed what God was doing that night when Gary opened up to me about the family picture five-year-old Sarah had drawn, the picture that left him out. At that moment I sensed God saying to me, "Changing Gary isn't your job; it's mine. Your job is to respond to my Spirit and choose to follow my ways even when you don't understand what I am doing. Your role isn't to change Gary; it's to love him." This insight changed my heart and helped transform our marriage.

God calls us to desire what he desires for us above all things. Are you struggling to see what God is doing in your marriage? Pray! Ask God to open your spiritual eyes to see where he is working in your circumstances. Admit to God your own hardheartedness. Confess any pride that may be blinding you to what he is doing. A tender and sensitive heart will be ready to respond to God at the slightest nudging. Then act on what he reveals to you. Live it out by loving your husband at the deepest possible level. As you guard your husband's heart, you and God are fighting a winning battle for your marriage.

KEYS FOR GUARDING HIS HEART

You are highly influential in your husband's life. You know him better than any other person in his life. You have a good grasp on his deepest needs, the quiet longings of his soul, his yearning for significance, the weaknesses he can hide from others but never from you. You can see his God-given strengths. Because of what you know, you can either help him or hinder him as he seeks to be the man, the husband, and the father God wants him to be. God has strategically placed you in his life to equip him, to influence him, to help mold his life, and to guard his heart.

Gary and I see it all the time: Much of a man's ability to be successful can be traced to the woman who whispers into his ear each night. He is naturally open to the influence of the love of his life. I'm not implying that a man's destiny is in the hands of his wife; it is not. Everyone is responsible for his or her own thoughts, words, life choices, and actions. But a man is vulnerable to his wife's influence.

Think about the next five years. How will your husband be

more alive, more fulfilled, more content, more successful as a result of your presence in his life? What about ten years down the road? Twenty? Don't leave the answer to chance. Determine to be the woman he needs, the co-guardian of his heart and your marriage. Commit yourself to be God's woman in his life, as described in Proverbs 31: "Who can find a virtuous and capable wife? She is worth more than precious rubies. Her husband can trust her, and she will greatly enrich his life. She will not hinder him but help him all her life" (vv. 10-12).

Couples all across the country have told Gary and me about their marriages and their needs. Based on what we have heard from thousands of men, I would like to share with you wives several specific keys for understanding your husband and guarding his heart from the temptation and pressures in a world hostile to Christian marriage.

Key 1: Help Him Achieve His Dreams

Someone once said, "If a woman is unhappy in her relationships, she can't concentrate on her work. If a man is unhappy at work, he can't focus on his relationships."[1] As you come to understand the significance of achievement, dreams, and goals in a man's life, you will be better equipped to guard his heart. And you will also benefit from this understanding because your husband's fulfillment in his work will free him to better nurture his relationship with you.

A man's wiring is complex, and it has been part of him since he was a boy. Think about it: If you have a son or a grandson, you know that he is wired to dream big. Every boy begins life with an energetic bounce in his step. He has his eye set on playing professional sports, being an astronaut, a firefighter, a brain surgeon, and a detective, sailing around the world, climbing Mt. Everest—all in one lifetime!

Or you may have a young man in your life who is in college and on the brink of conquering the world. He dreams of making a million dollars before turning thirty, owning his own fleet of cross-country trucks, building the tallest skyscrapers in town, writing a best-selling novel, or wiping out crime in the community. He is full of drive and determination. He's going to make his mark in the world or die trying.

Your husband was once a little boy and then a young man brimming with big dreams. Where is he today? Has he stopped dreaming? If so, when did it happen and why? Should a man ever quit dreaming? I don't think so. When the dreams die, a part of the man dies. You can guard your husband's heart against death of soul not only by connecting to his plans and his drive to accomplish but also by helping him achieve his dreams.

A man's dreams and his search for identity are closely intertwined with what he does. Men derive an enormous amount of their self-esteem from their work. And when the job is no longer a challenge, when the routine or the pressures or the hassles dampen the dream, a man may need a career change. He may be ready to start over, take a cut in pay, and risk failure just to follow his dream.

How many times do we wives panic at thoughts of a pay cut or starting over? Perhaps you are one of them. At the risk of losing financial security and earning power, you say, "Hold on! There's no way we can start over!" And so his dream dies. But ask yourself this question: If taking a salary cut would bring my husband a deepened sense of purpose, allowing him to find enjoyment in life and ultimately pushing him closer to God, wouldn't it be worth it? Too many men live with regrets of what they could have done. Don't let your husband be one of them.

Are you willing to come alongside your husband and listen to his goals and what he longs to accomplish in life? Do your words and attitudes toward his dreams empower him, or are you holding him back out of your own fear and insecurity?

How can you discover your husband's dreams and strategize to help him achieve them? Here are a number of suggestions:

Be prayerful. I love Psalm 37:4: "Take delight in the Lord, and he will give you your heart's desires." Stay close to the Lord in prayer. Let God into your heart, and tell him how you long to help your husband discover new career opportunities that will fulfill his dreams. Tell your husband that you long for God's best for him and that you are committed to seeking God with him about the next step in his career path.

Be alert to the activities that bring him joy. Does he like what he is doing? Do his training and skills line up with his life goals and dreams? Would other careers or positions bring him greater fulfillment? If you don't know, ask him.

Help him gain the training, skills, or degree that will equip him for fulfilling work. This may mean volunteering to work longer hours or cutting back expenses so he can take some classes. Let him know that you will do whatever it takes to help him follow God's leading in his career.

Believe in him. Gary thrives on my belief in him. When I remind him of all the reasons I believe in him, I am just holding up a mirror for him, showing him the man God has made him to be. I am convinced that the most important way of demonstrating my support in Gary's life is to express to him daily my genuine belief in him as a man. I say things like, "Go for it, Gary. I believe in you. You know I'm your biggest fan." Your affirmation of belief in your husband's calling and purpose can rekindle hope that has died and ignite the fire of purpose and his passion for life.

Respect him. The bottom line is this: Your husband may have the respect of others, but he needs to know that you respect him. With your confidence in his decisions, he can face any obstacle. Tell him, "What you are doing is important. I see how much you put into that project. And I appreciate how hard you work to provide for our family." When you verbalize your respect, your words will help build your husband's confidence as a man.

Encourage him. Your husband has a logical, problem-solving mind. Whether he is entering the boardroom at work or the basement at home, he is looking for something to fix. And his brain doesn't take vacation. Sometimes the tasks, relationships, and problems of everyday life tear him down and *dis*courage him because not every problem can be solved. You can be a refreshing presence and voice to build him up and *en*courage—to breathe courage into—him. As you discuss your day together, look for opportunities to affirm him: "Honey, I'm so proud of the way you handled your boss's criticism"; "Your work is really making a difference, even if others don't notice"; "You are such a caring husband and father. The kids and I are so blessed." Remind him that you are grateful for, and thank God for, his character qualities and the wisdom he shows in making tough decisions all day long.

Key 2: Be Alert to Controlling Tendencies

On a recent trip to the West Coast, Gary and I were driving down one of our favorite streets in San Francisco, looking for a new restaurant we had heard about. At one point I uttered three seemingly harmless words: "Let's ask directions." But what Gary heard was something completely different. My simple suggestion sounded to him like a challenge of his ability, as if I had said, "You'll never find this place on your own."

One of the most destructive torpedoes to a marriage relationship is a wife's intentional or unintentional attempt to control her husband. Michelle Weiner-Davis writes: "A man has radar for anything that smells of control. The need to be self-determined is an incredibly powerful force in his life. They want to be in charge of themselves. Men often feel weak if they accept influence or advice from others. Research suggests that men's number-one complaint about their wife is trying to change them. Guys don't appreciate this nurturing quality in us. They feel nagged, controlled, and hen-pecked and stubbornly resist even the most benevolent advice."[2]

I have learned that it is better not to offer a man advice unless he asks for it. Tell your husband that you have confidence in his ability to work things out. Many times that statement alone will erode his wall of defensiveness and open him to ask for advice or help.

And yet there are times when we can't afford to tiptoe around a husband's sensitivity to control if an important issue needs to be addressed. For example, if your husband turns the wrong way on a one-way street, he needs your advice—immediately! When these kinds of occasions arise, help him understand that you are not criticizing him, and encourage him not to take your contribution personally.

Another way wives tend to control their husbands is by taking over the household. Michelle Weiner-Davis says, "Relationships are like seesaws. The more one person does of something, the less the other person does of it. This holds true for about everything. If you put the kids to bed every night, your partner won't. If you are a tidiness freak, your partner is probably a slob. We balance each other out. Just like a seesaw. The more we do, the less they do."[3]

There are things I really enjoy about taking care of our home, such as the cooking and the laundry. But I tend to assume full responsibility for handling everything. When I install myself as the resident expert, I condition Gary to think I can do it all—which, of course, I can't. For example, if I'm getting ready for company, I sometimes start complaining about the pressure of doing it all. My complaining comes across as controlling to Gary.

If you want to see your husband more involved in responsibilities at home, the change must begin with you. Back off from being a know-it-all, do-it-all controller. Give him room to step in and assume some responsibilities with the chores and kids.

Key 3: Love Him Unconditionally

Not long ago we received a letter from Becky, a radio listener. Her husband, Roland, is in the Air Force and currently deployed overseas. Becky stated that Roland is a hard man to live with at times. He has been very critical of her, making her feel unappreciated. He has even been so by long distance—in his letters and phone calls. For the last several months, Becky and the kids have been getting along very well without Roland—almost too well. But this time apart has also helped Becky realize how she needs to love her husband, faults and all.

She told us, "I am learning to love Roland the way Christ loves us: by looking past his faults to meet his needs. When I do that, I am helping him reach his potential as a man and as my husband. I realize that he needs to be needed, especially now that we are living without him. So when he becomes critical in a letter or over the phone, I reaffirm his role in the family and how much we miss him. Instead of reacting to his words, I tell him I love him and appreciate his sacrifice for the family. When he falls short in his own eyes, I remind him that he has a wife who still thinks the world of him, understands him, and loves him unconditionally."

Unconditional love is vitally important because it mirrors the love Christ has for us. He loves us, mistakes and all. While we were in a sinful state, full of guilt and shame, Christ died on the cross for us (see Romans 5:8). That's unconditional love, the very love that was modeled at the Cross, the kind of love that accepts me just as I am. Every one of us longs to be loved this way. We ache for acceptance that comes with no pressure to perform. Your husband longs for the freedom to be fully who he is, assured that his wife will stand beside him through it all.

Love your husband unconditionally by letting him need you. Every morning I wake up to these gently whispered words, "Barb, I need you." These are words from a man's soul, words that encompass the most vulnerable point of our relational world. These words connect Gary and me each morning. Your husband needs you too, although he may not know how to verbalize it.

During one of our conferences, I spoke to a woman who managed a family business with her husband. She was bright, attractive, and loaded with talent. She and her husband had three kids. But she admitted to me that she had neglected her husband's need for her. A female employee stepped in to meet that need, first by complimenting his broad shoulders, becoming his cheerleader, and eventually meeting his sexual needs.

Don't let another woman usurp your God-given role of meeting your husband's needs. You are a wise and loving wife if you welcome those needs and give yourself to meet them.

Key 4: Respect His Differences

Men and women are wired differently. You have probably heard of many of the common differences between men and women. In general, men are more solution-oriented, more logical, less emotional, less verbal, and more single-focused. Men define their masculinity through separateness; women define femininity through attachment.

Men tend to analyze and process issues internally. When

they do talk to each other, men use "*report* talk," communicating in a condensed, edited format, skipping many of the details in order to get to the bottom line. Women, however, are wired for "*rapport* talk." Details are important to us. Women often process verbally. Somehow the thinking, hearing, and speaking are interrelated, and we need all three working at once to express ourselves fully.

One of the most significant male-female differences is in the brain. Recent studies on the brain give us many answers to these differences. Scientific evidence suggests that physiological and neurological differences between men and women begin long before birth.

As you probably know, the brain is divided into two hemispheres. The left side of the brain is characterized as logical, mathematical, factual, analytical, and practical. The right side of the brain is creative, artistic, intuitive, holistic, multiprocessing, and perceptive of emotion. These two hemispheres are connected by the corpus callosum, a fibrous cable allowing both sides to communicate with each other.

At about the sixteenth week of development, the brain of the male fetus is washed with a hormone called androgen. At this time, many of the fibrous connections in the corpus callosum begin to dissolve, limiting the communication from hemisphere to hemisphere. As a result, about 80 percent of all males use only one side of their brain at a time. The female fetus does not experience the androgen wash, so women are born with all interconnecting fibers in tact. Simply put, the male brain is not designed to communicate between hemispheres as the female brain is.

Here is one practical expression of this male-female difference: "Men's brains are highly compartmentalized and have the ability to separate and retain information. At the end of a long day, a man's brain can file them all away. The female brain cannot store information like this—the problems keep going around in her head. The only way for her to get them out is to talk through and acknowledge them. Therefore, when a woman talks at the end of the day, her objective is to discharge the problems, not find solutions or conclusions."[4]

Another significant difference between you and your husband is in the area of emotional expression. Dr. John Gottman, marriage researcher and psychologist, explains: "From early childhood, boys learn to suppress their emotions, while girls learn to express and manage a complete range of feelings. A man is more likely to equate being emotional with weakness and vulnerability because he has been raised to suppress rather than voice what he feels. Meanwhile, women have spent their early years learning how to verbalize all kinds of emotions. In order to fully understand why husbands and wives so often miss each other's needs, we have to recognize that the sexes may be physically programmed to react differently to emotional conflict—beginning in childhood."[5]

You may have been taught that feelings, nurture, care, and love are ingredients to a healthy relationship. Your husband probably didn't get that message. But you are well equipped to be his best teacher in the skill of connecting emotionally.

In addition to these obvious differences between men and women, you need to understand your man's unique makeup. Study him, listen to him, and communicate with him. Ask him what his greatest needs are. The more you understand your husband's male characteristics, the more you can access his deep need for you and effectively meet those needs. Here are a few basic guidelines for meeting him where he lives.

Communicate openly with him. Sometimes when I get upset about something, I pull in and stop talking instead of telling

Gary what's bothering me. That's really not fair. Our husbands are not mind readers. Tell your husband honestly and clearly what is on your mind and in your heart. And when he is talking, work on giving him your undivided attention. He needs you to listen to him.

Give your husband time to process his feelings, allowing his thoughts to move from his head to his heart and then into words. Work on creating a safe environment in which he can express himself at his pace. Real love allows room for differing styles of communication and differing ways to process. The goal is to discover a process through which he can share his hopes, his dreams, and his failures, knowing he will still be accepted.

Let him feel your touch. Think about how you feel when you see your husband playing with the kids. Don't you feel warm, cared for, safe? This is how he feels toward you when you reach out to him with loving touch. He feels close to you.

One morning I arrived at our office at nine o'clock. Gary had been there since seven o'clock, and he was already in hyperdrive. He called me into his office to look over some papers he wanted me to work on. He was all business, and that's all he wanted from me at the moment. As I stood behind him at the desk, I placed my hands on his back and began to gently massage the tightness out of his neck and shoulders. In less than a minute the papers dropped from his hand to the desk, and he relaxed in my hands. I could feel the tension drain out of him. After a few minutes, I scooped up the papers, thanked him for the help, and went to work.

That morning Gary made at least three unnecessary trips into my office. He was more relaxed than usual, winking at me, smiling. Just a few minutes of gentle, loving touch had transformed him from a nose-to-the-grindstone executive to a contented and congenial partner.

Every marriage needs lots of healthy, appropriate touch—even when it is not leading up to sex. You can meet that need in your husband through hugs, pats on the back, holding hands, even a back rub at the end of a day. Touch helps men to feel loved and worthy. When you are giving your husband this kind of blessing, you are protecting him from temptations in the world by meeting one of his greatest needs.

Understand his sexual needs. Hormones are not just a female issue. Hormonal chemistry influences both women *and* men, and both sexes experience emotional highs and lows because of hormones.

A woman's hormonal cycle is well documented. For twenty-one days after menstruation, estrogen is plentiful, providing women with a sense of well-being and a generally positive attitude. But during the next seven days, that level drops dramatically—and so does our mood! Many of us tend to become grouchy and more easily irritated during the week before menstruation.

Did you know that your husband is "hormonal" as well? "He is wired for physiological release," states Dr. Kevin Leman. "Sexual desire is largely a matter of hormones for your husband. The level of testosterone varies from man to man. You may have a twenty-four-hour husband, a forty-eight-hour husband, or a once-every-five-days husband. But every man has a clock that is counting the minutes until the next sexual release. Eventually he is going to feel he needs a sexual experience. I can't overstate this too much because your body is wired so different. For a man, sexual desire is physically based and ever present."[6]

Sometimes you may be interested in sex, but the routine from a stressful life can knock the interest right out of you. At the same time, you realize that your husband's sexual alarm is sounding. If you have been drained emotionally and you have nothing to give, sometimes you have to say no. But in the next breath make sure to tell him yes for tomorrow night. That way he knows the end is in sight! Then as you look forward to it, save up your energy.

To your husband, sex is a means of communication and an attempt to become one with you spiritually, emotionally, and physically. In fact, sex is often a barometer of how things are going in other areas of your relationship. When communication is good and healthy growth is happening, you tend to celebrate by enjoying each other sexually. And he is usually ready to celebrate anytime and anywhere!

You have a tremendous opportunity to tell him how wonderful and worthy he is by meeting his sexual needs. You may not realize how much you do for your husband by welcoming his advances. When you receive him with a heart full of joy, you can build up his sense of worth, causing him to feel desirable and acceptable. Notice how the bride in the following verses eagerly anticipates a romantic interlude: "I am my lover's, the one he desires. Come, my love, let us go out into the fields and spend the night among the wildflowers. Let us get up early and go out to the vineyards. Let us see whether the vines have budded, whether the blossoms have opened, and whether the pomegranates are in flower. And there I will give you my love" (Song of Songs 7:10-12).

Take a lesson from this wife. Do you hear the excitement in her voice? She is delighted to be alone with her husband! You don't hear any whining, such as, "Do we have to?" or "I'm too tired." This woman knows she is married to a winner, and she is wise enough to express it within the exclusive bonds of marriage.

Look your best for him. Men are visually "on point" most of the time. Your husband is attracted to beauty and stimulated sexually when he sees it—especially if that beauty is you! Outside the home, he probably encounters plenty of women each day who are well dressed and beautiful. When you take the time and have the attitude to look sharp, your husband will take notice.

Your clothes, your hair, your skin, your weight, your nails, your fragrance—it's all you, and your husband notices when you're attending to these details and when you're not. You want to take care of yourself because it makes you feel great. But your husband needs you to take care of yourself because there are plenty of other women around him who do.

Key 5: Help Provide Companionship

We all need encouragement from others, and men and women share encouragement differently. Men tend to encourage each other as friends with a high five or on the sports field with a friendly slap on the behind. When a woman needs encouragement, she goes for a hug from her supportive friends. We need an emotional connection for companionship. For us, it hasn't been a good time if we haven't had a good laugh or cry together. For men, companionship is more a matter of doing something together—playing a game, finishing a project, hunting prey, watching a movie, etc. Men don't generally have lengthy conversations on the phone about the details of their lives. They can be comfortable with periods of silence.

Men need other men to help them fight their everyday battles, whether it is troubleshooting an electrical short, planning a career move, or just getting feedback on maintaining integrity in the workplace. They also need male companions who will challenge them to follow God and grow as spiritual leaders in the home. Your husband needs a band of brothers, like-minded Christian men who look beyond themselves and their circumstances to seek the counsel of God.

Encourage your husband to hang out with other men who are interested in Bible study groups and accountability groups in which he can develop his skills as a leader in the home. Proverbs 27:17 states, "As iron sharpens iron, a friend sharpens a friend." One of the best things you can do for your husband and for yourself is to encourage your husband's relationships, which will sharpen him as a man of God, a husband, and a father.

He also needs *you* to be his friend. As we have surveyed men and women across the country, we find that men have a high need for companionship from their wives. Husband-wife companionship means that we speak the truth to one another in love and are quick to forgive. We remain honest with our feelings and settle conflicts quickly. But keep in mind that your husband isn't your girlfriend. At times you may get offended with him simply because he acts like a man. Then he gets ticked off because you get teary-eyed and emotional and act like a woman!

Companionship with your husband also means that you enter his world of interests and join him in some of them. Someone once gave me a card that read: "What women want: To be loved, to be listened to, to be desired, to be respected, to be needed, to be trusted, and sometimes just to be held. What men want: Tickets to the World Series!" What does your husband like to do: go bowling, go fishing, or work in his shop in the garage? You will meet his needs when you find ways to participate in his areas of interest.

While I was at lunch with friends awhile back, one woman mentioned that her husband had found a "boating buddy." Another woman exclaimed, "Girl, *you* need to be his boating buddy!" She went on to tell us that she plays in a volleyball league with her husband and works out with him at the gym. She even went hunting with him once.

"Did you shoot the gun?" someone asked.

"No, I sat in the car with a book when he was out in the field," she explained. "But we had a great day riding through the country and talking."

Another couple I know took up playing tennis together. The husband told his wife, "This is what I always thought marriage would be like." I know a number of women who golf with their husbands. Good friends of ours own a Harley Davidson, which they ride together.

Encouraging your husband's friendships and being his best friend is essential to defending your marriage. This may mean sacrificing some of your time and interests, but it is a gift that your husband will always cherish and that will draw you closer as a couple.

Key 6: Recognize Your Powerful Role

Never underestimate the role of a woman in her husband's life. God created us to enjoy this magnificent union called marriage. In Genesis, he refers to the first woman as a "helper" to her husband. Here is something very amazing. The Hebrew word translated "helper" in Genesis 2:18 (NIV) is more accurately translated "completer." Elsewhere in the Old Testament this word is always used in reference to God himself. This means you occupy a position of dignity, honor, and incredible value in your husband's life!

The completer role leads us to a better understanding of a woman's distinctive strengths in the marriage relationship. You complete your husband as no one else can. Think about it: Whenever we need help with something, we go to someone who is more proficient than we are, someone who is stronger in that area. Sometimes our husbands complete us by stretching us and supplying the help we need. But we are also created to be that someone for our husbands.

How do women complete their husbands? There are many ways, and the variations with each are as diverse as your two personalities. One way is by helping your husband fulfill his dreams, as we talked about earlier in this chapter. For example, your husband may not have a clear idea of what he wants to do with his life. You complete him by praying for him and with him, being a sounding board for his ideas, contributing suggestions based on your knowledge of his skills and interests, helping him sort through options, and encouraging him.

Also, women generally possess keener emotional sensitivity than men, able to pick up on unspoken messages, kind of like radar or a sixth sense. I can't really explain this capacity or gift, but most of you women know what I'm talking about. You complete your husband when you use this God-given trait to minister to hurts that might otherwise be overlooked.

For example, one day many years ago our daughter Sarah arrived home from elementary school and was uncharacteristically quiet. She gave me a brief rundown of her day and then slipped silently off to her room. My spirit was uneasy. I knew in my heart there was more Sarah needed to share. Gary witnessed our conversation, but he didn't sense what I did. I told Gary what I thought, and he spent some time with Sarah. As we followed up on my hunch, we learned from Sarah that some girls at school had been pretty tough on her that day, and she was hurting. Gary's ministry to Sarah that day would have been incomplete without my insight.

A man often relies on logical reasoning rather than the intuitive senses. Your gift of sensitivity equips you to help your husband gain a more complete picture. You are also more adept at developing relationships and enjoying deep, intimate communication. These traits help you view family decisions based on their impact on people and relationships. For example, your husband may think it more important to spend Saturday afternoon organizing the garage than attending the wedding of a coworker's daughter. You can help him see the importance of honoring the relationship with your presence. You complete your husband by helping him be more people-centered and not too focused on the task side.

Another way to complete your husband as a helper is to let him lead in the home. Many husbands Gary and I talk to suffer from low self-esteem, feeling they just don't measure up to the role of leader. By relinquishing any control you may be exerting in your marriage and affirming him as God's leader, you can bolster your husband's self-esteem.

I want Gary to lead our home, but let's face it, sometimes I want things to go my way! A power struggle wages within me. At times I think it would be a breeze to lead our home. But truthfully, God didn't intend for women to bear the weight of the entire household. Women were not created to lead the home. The New Testament clearly states, "A husband is the head of his wife as Christ is the head of his body, the church" (Ephesians 5:23). You must trust God and his plan for your family. When you do, you will free your husband to be the leader God wants him to be.

You can also complete your husband by helping him relate to your children and be their hero. The bond between mother and child is usually strong because they spend more time together and mothers tend to be more relational. Being largely task oriented, your husband may be more concerned with the kids' behavior. He needs your help in bonding with his kids. Give him your insight when your child is going through stress. Teach him to be understanding, compassionate, gentle, and patient with these impressionable little people. He may not realize it, but the way he cares for them contributes to the development of their personalities.

Encourage your husband to spend time alone with each child. They need to see where he works and understand what he does there. Suggest that he take a child along when he runs to the hardware store or takes the car for a fill-up. Some of life's best lessons can be learned in these casual, unstructured moments of interacting.

Key 7: Be Committed to Your Husband

Call me old-fashioned, but when I said, "I will love you, honor you, and cherish you until death do us part," I meant it. The foundation of marriage, a sacred institution, is cemented by the notion of permanence. Both husband and wife must be committed to an everlasting bond. Otherwise, it is only a contractual arrangement that either can dissolve if he or she gets distracted.

Make a commitment to be the woman of only one man: your husband. You may be thinking, *Barb, I did that on my wedding day.* Yes, and so did I. But in a divorce-proof marriage, this commitment must be affirmed and lived out daily. It is so easy in our culture to get distracted by other men. There is always the temptation to think the grass is greener across the fence: "Her husband is so spiritual"; "That man is a real leader in their home"; "What I could do with the bucks he earns"; "Wow, what a good-looking guy!" When you wake up every morning, recommit yourself to the man you married. You will be better equipped to deal with these temptations.

Where do these tempting thoughts lead? Into illicit affairs, first emotional and then physical. Whenever a woman gives her heart away, her emotions follow. And emotional wandering is just a dress rehearsal for the real show: adultery. You may be blinded by your emotions into thinking it could never happen to you. That's a myth Satan is all too happy to perpetuate. It *can* happen to you. It *is* happening to women just like you. You must earnestly "take captive every thought to make it obedient to Christ" (2 Corinthians 10:5, NIV). Commit to being your husband's devoted wife, then put every contrary impulse in jail and throw away the key!

Your commitment of faithfulness to your husband must flow from your preeminent commitment to Jesus Christ. Keep the living Lord present in your heart and your home. He is the key to unlocking the treasure of your husband's heart. "[The Lord] will be your sure foundation, providing a rich store of salvation, wisdom, and knowledge. The fear of the Lord is the key to this treasure" (Isaiah 33:6).

Your husband and family tap into you for a variety of needs, and this can be exhausting. There is not enough of you to go around unless you acquire strength from outside yourself. The Lord promises to strengthen the weary, to increase the power of the weak. "He gives power to those who are tired and worn out; he offers strength to the weak. Even youths will become exhausted, and young men will give up. But those who wait on the Lord will find new strength. They will fly high on wings like eagles. They will run and not grow weary. They will walk and not faint" (Isaiah 40:29-31).

Your husband needs you as his soul mate in following Christ. But you cannot share what you do not have. You must be pursuing your own personal relationship with Christ. Only by nurturing your own spiritual life will you have something to share with your husband.

Read the Word. Get into a Bible study group with other women, and draw from their experiences of walking with God. Fortifying yourself in God's presence and power will help you guard your heart. And protected hearts are prepared to battle victoriously with the enemy. A woman whose source of strength is in Christ is ready and able to do what God requires of her.

Pray about everything. With God, no subject is off-limits. He is interested in the smallest areas of your life—and the biggest ones too. Pray with your husband. Few experiences are as intimate as that of a husband and wife baring their souls before God and one another.

Keep in stride with each other. You both need a burning passion to follow Christ at all costs. As you pursue God together as a couple, he can powerfully use you to have an impact on your children, your friends, your parents, your community, and your world.

Point your husband to Christ. If your husband does not know the living Lord, help your partner to meet the Savior. If he has already given his life to the Lord, keep pointing him to the only source of wisdom and strength. Don't give up on your husband's spiritual potential. You can give to your husband in many different ways, but the most lasting gift is that of placing Christ in the center of your marriage. God can fulfill his purpose in your husband's life when you are at his side, strengthening him, encouraging him, and guarding his heart.

Chapter Twelve

GUARD YOUR WIFE'S HEART

WE'RE TALKING MAN TO MAN IN THIS CHAPTER, SO I WANT TO level with you about a couple of things. First I want to fire my parting shot on your need for support in your mission to guard your heart and home. Then I want to leave you with seven vital keys for guarding your wife's heart. For sure, if you don't follow through on the first topic, you will have difficulty following through on the second.

YOU NEED STOUT-HEARTED MEN

God wants you to win in your role as husband and father in your family. But he's not going to do everything for you. You have to step up to the plate in his strength and do what he gives you to do. God wants you to bring every resource to bear in order to attain the goal of guarding the hearts of your wife and children. And that means taking the risk to reach out for help and encouragement.

Men need each other. We were designed for companionship, not isolation. When we are alone, we run the risk of being overwhelmed by life. When we team up with at least one other man, we are able to defend ourselves against the threats to our marriages. Solomon said, "A person standing alone can be attacked and defeated, but two can stand back-to-back and conquer. Three are even better, for a triple-braided cord is not easily broken" (Ecclesiastes 4:12). Two or three men bonded together in fellowship and companionship are better able to fight off the pain and challenges of everyday life better than each one by himself.

Yet what do we often see around us? Men trying to do it alone, men who claim they don't need anyone else. These guys isolate themselves from others, including their wives, kids, friends, parents, neighbors, and church family. They put up walls around themselves and suffer the natural result: loneliness. This is not God's desire. He wants us to relate to each other, depend on each other, and support each other.

This truth finally got through my own thick skull when I was in crisis with my family. As a young husband and father, I began attending breakfast with a few guys from my church. About a dozen of us would meet weekly to encourage each other, study the Word together, and uphold each other in prayer. The group fizzled after several months, but my need for that kind of support didn't. I finally got up the guts to ask three of the guys to keep meeting with me. I knew I needed help. So the four of us continued.

We read and discussed Christian books to stretch us as men, husbands, and dads. We prayed for each other. At times our sessions were pretty heavy; at other times we did a lot of laughing. Through it all our hearts began to knit together. And we're still getting together more than twenty-four years later. I don't know how I would have made it without them.

In 1992 the four of us traveled together to Boulder, Colorado, for the Promise Keepers conference. One night after the meeting, I and my little band of amigos stayed up late and really got down to business. We decided to grant each other permission to ask the tough questions of life—and to answer them truthfully. We agreed to hold each other accountable when we got home—not in order to condemn each other but to pray for each other and challenge each other to obedience and growth.

These are the kinds of questions I'm talking about:

- ⊕ How's your thought life been this week?
- ⊕ How are you handling the balance between work and home?
- ⊕ Have you been in the Word over the last few days?
- ⊕ What has God been teaching you recently?
- ⊕ How are you doing in handling God's provision of time, talent, and money?
- ⊕ Are you being responsible to protect your eyes, hands, feet, and mind when you are around women other than your wife?
- ⊕ Are you shooting straight in answering the above questions, or are you blowing smoke?

Do you have a friend or group of friends in your life willing to ask you the tough questions? Or do you and your buddies talk only about the local team, the newest fishing lure, or politics whenever you get together? Are you tight with some men who love you enough not only to celebrate your successes but also to stand by you in your failures? Do they stick close during bad times as well as good times without falling into the trap of telling you only what you want to hear? Much of the success of my ministry to my own family can be traced to the guys who have kept me honest over the years by holding me accountable.

Little did we know that what the four of us were getting into would grow into a long-standing ministry for men called CrossTrainers. Today about six hundred men in central Iowa meet weekly to study the Word, pray for each other, and hold each other accountable. CrossTrainers is based on the premise that a man needs to crosstrain in five areas of relationship: with Christ, with his wife, with his kids, with his friends, with his community. A CrossTrainer guards his heart. A CrossTrainer is on the alert for frontal attacks as well as sneak attacks. A CrossTrainer not only starts the race of faith but also finishes it well.

A CrossTrainer is a warrior, a man willing to stand in the line of fire with his brothers. He's willing to march alongside other men in a culture determined to pick off anyone who holds a righteous standard. A CrossTrainer is willing to stand for something more important than his own selfish desires. He's the kind of guy who not only quotes 1 Corinthians 16:13-14 but also *lives* it: "Be on guard. Stand true to what you believe. Be courageous. Be strong. And everything you do must be done with love."

Most strategically, a CrossTrainer knows he can't do it alone. He knows he will make it only in the company of some faithful buddies who are committed to him and to each other. He knows a cord of three strands is not easily broken.

You don't have to be in one of our CrossTrainer groups to be a CrossTrainer kind of man. You just need to join forces with a handful of men who are determined to guard their hearts together as God intended them to do. What's holding you back?

STANDING GUARD OVER YOUR DEAREST

As a husband, you have been called by God to love your wife as Christ loves the church. A significant part of loving your wife is guarding her heart from the enemies of your marriage. Here are seven keys to guarding your wife's heart.

Key 1: Ask, Listen, and Connect

I want to share with you a question that will save you a lot of guesswork and grief with your wife; it's a question my friend Charlie taught me. Whenever she is facing a problem or a struggle, whenever she comes to you with a complaint or a worry, ask the following question, then listen carefully to her answer and connect with her by meeting her need: "What do you need from me right now: sympathy or a solution?" If you don't ask or if you ask and fail to listen with your heart to her reply, you may try to fix something when all she wants from you is emotional support. Or you may do nothing when she is looking for you to step in and help her solve a problem.

Women are wired differently from men emotionally. When something trips a breaker in a your wife's life and the emotions bubble over, you may be tempted to try to fix it, to tell your wife what to do. At that point, however, she may not want to hear anything that sounds remotely like a solution. She just needs you to be with her through the range of feelings she is experiencing. She needs your sympathy and comfort. Save the advice until she's had a chance to express her heart, and then think even harder about saving it until she asks!

Real connection between you and your wife happens when you engage her heart by asking what she is feeling and validating that she is struggling with something. For example, she comes home from work in tears because of a conflict with one of her colleagues. Don't jump in with something like, "Just don't have lunch with her anymore," or even worse, "If you would do it my way, you wouldn't have these conflicts." You may only add to her hurt, especially if it sounds as if you're trying to fix *her*. Instead, say to your wife, "Tell me what you're feeling." Then after she tells you, respond by saying something like, "Honey, I know you're hurting. What do you need from me: a hug, some space, or some feedback?"

Have you ever just held your wife when she was struggling with a problem? I tried it recently when Barb was stressed. I just looked at her and said, "May I hold you?" She melted in my arms. I couldn't believe it. After several minutes and a few tissues, she looked at me and said, "Thanks, Gary, for supporting me." I was stunned. It worked!

A wife who feels connected to you through your sensitivity to her emotions is a wife with a guarded heart.

Key 2: Offer Practical Help

Who does which chores around your house? Perhaps you have it all mapped out, even down to written job descriptions. One fairly traditional division of labor Barb and I run into goes something like this:

- ⊕ Husband—provides most of the family's income, does the yard work, maintains the car, fixes anything that's broken
- ⊕ Wife—provides most of the child care, does the housework, maintains the family's social calendar, fixes the meals

Your formal or informal job description may be just the opposite of this example. More than likely, it is some kind of blend of tasks. In reality, there is no wrong way to divide up the day-to-day work of being a family—provided that you and your wife are in agreement about it. But a key to guarding your wife's heart is to help her in practical ways with whatever work she has to do. And at some seasons in your life, she may need you to kick it up a notch and take on more responsibility, especially if she is working outside the home. Sometimes when your wife is fixing a meal, she may need you to step in and help out by setting the table, peeling potatoes, or just asking, "What can I do to help you?" Believe me, as you offer and provide practical help, she'll think you are wonderful! But truthfully, that's what a godly man does. He scouts out creative and practical ways to serve his wife. He takes the initiative. He serves.

Your practical help can extend beyond the front door of your house. If your wife is in charge of decorating a banquet at church, sign on to be her "gofer"—carrying tables, stringing lights, or whatever. If she has a rush project at work, see what you can do to lighten her load. If she has a responsibility at your kids' school, join in and share that responsibility with her as your time and skills allow. Anytime you can step in to offer practical assistance, you will fortify your wife's heart and your marriage.

Our daughter Sarah married a rock-solid man named Scott. We don't call him a son-in-law; to us he's a son, and we love him dearly. When their first child—our first grandchild—was born recently, Barb stayed with them for a week to help out cooking meals, doing laundry, and changing Mason's diapers. Except she didn't get much of a chance to change diapers. Scott very respectfully stepped in, saying he didn't want to miss out on anything with his son, even the bonding that comes from changing his diapers. Sarah didn't change a diaper for three weeks. Scott remains a warrior at seeking to guard her heart by providing practical help with their son.

God intended that children have two parents for a reason. It's tough for a mom to go one-on-one with an energetic child, much less get double- or triple-teamed by other kids in need. You can protect your wife's heart from a heap of bitterness and resentment if you pitch in and help with the kids. Dying to self-ishness is lived out by serving your wife in the day-to-day

chores. Don't save your practical help only for special occasions; make it an everyday occurrence. There is wisdom in the
familiar kitchen motto informing us that the secret passageway
to a woman's heart runs right through the daily chores: "I like
hugs and I like kisses, but what I need right now is help with the
dishes."

Key 3: Make Time Just for Her

Do you know why some women are lured away from their husbands into extramarital affairs? It's usually not because she
found someone smarter, stronger, handsomer, or wealthier
than her husband. Some of these factors may play a role, but the
big draw is often that these women discover someone who gives
them the time and attention their husbands never provided.

You must guard your wife's heart by giving her the focus and
attention that won her for you in the first place. If you don't
meet your wife's need for friendship and emotional intimacy,
you will leave her vulnerable to any man who will. Or your wife
may try to fill that need in other ways that are more socially acceptable. She may fill the void you leave in her life by seeking
companionship from your children, her friends, or her coworkers. When she is hurting or has a problem, she may turn to
someone else who is more sympathetic and understanding. The
less you fill the role of soul mate in her life, the less interested
she will be in you sexually and in every other way.

If you sense that your wife is withdrawing from you, something is very wrong. She is no longer willing to connect with
you, probably because you have not demonstrated willingness
to connect with her emotionally by giving her your time and attention. If you do not deal with this problem, your marriage is in
serious danger of divorce—if not the physical, legal kind, at
least emotional divorce. Some women begin to look for an exit

because they feel hopeless and unfulfilled in a setting that may never change.

Dan got the picture just in time. Here was a man who had fallen into the trap of letting work run his life. In the process he was losing his wife, Karen. He tried a number of times to cut back his hours, but another big deal always came up, and time with Karen was pushed to the back burner.

Then one day at work he got a pink slip. In an hour's time, everything he had given his life to was reduced to the contents of the cardboard box he carried out to his car when he left. He was suddenly jobless. But this hard blow served to interrupt the downhill slide of Dan and Karen's marriage. They had plenty of time to talk. Dan realized the damage he had caused by neglecting his wife. He set himself to repairing the damage by devoting more attention to Karen.

Six months later, Dan regarded his dismissal as a gift from God, a second chance at giving Karen the time and attention she deserves. He knew that he would eventually find another job— and he did. But he was deeply grateful that he didn't have to find another wife. And Karen is rejoicing that she has her husband back.

Don't let your vocation or avocations, as important as they are, cause you to leave your wife's heart unguarded. Determine to give her the intimate time and attention she needs.

Key 4: Give Her Time for Herself

Barb graduated from Drake University with a degree in art. She is deeply gifted, but more important, she is refreshed and re-charged as she paints and writes. While we were raising our children, Barb was creative in many ways in our home and with the kids, but her own art was placed on the back burner. I wasn't as good as I could have been about allowing my wife time and opportunity to follow her dreams in this area.

But now that our daughters are grown, we decided to do something about making Barb's dream for her own art and writing studio a reality. We sold the functional family home where the girls grew up and built our dream home. When we were in the planning stages, I said to Barb, "Let's make a room in the house just for you, a studio where you can paint and write. I want you to have some time and a place to just create."

You should have seen the smile on her face! And that's just what we did. Today Barb's studio is a room we built over the garage, a room looking out over the treetops, just up the stairs from her dream kitchen. I find her burrowed into her studio early in the morning, starting her day by spending time alone with God. She is thrilled to have her own space for exercising her creativity.

You are a wise, guarding husband if you make sure your wife has time and opportunity to rejuvenate herself. This may mean that you watch the kids one evening a week while she attends a women's Bible study group, goes out with her girlfriends, works out at the gym, or just takes a long, quiet walk by herself. It may mean perusing the community college catalog with her, helping her find an interesting class to take. It may mean spending some money to get her the potting wheel she's always wanted. Study her to discover what makes her come alive in her free time, then do whatever you can to feed that joy.

Key 5: Love Her Unconditionally

Lanny was something of a neat freak, and he expected his wife, Dee, to be the same. He wanted the house sparkling clean when he arrived home from work every day, even though their four kids made this demand virtually impossible. He wanted Dee and the kids to put everything away after use, but it seldom happened. What's more, he wanted his wife to go the gym and get her pre-children figure back. But Dee had neither the motivation nor the energy for pumping iron. Frustrated, Lanny wrote up his expectations and posted them for Dee to see.

To her credit, Dee had tried to do what Lanny wanted. But "the list" was the last straw. She ripped it down and handed it to him. "Honey, I can't do all this," she said firmly. "I don't have the time or the energy. And even if I did, I can't meet your lofty standards. Besides, I don't think our home needs to be as clean as a hospital operating room all the time. I do the best I can to keep things shipshape around here. If you want it better than that, you'll just have to do the rest yourself."

Lanny tried to argue the point, but Dee held up her hand to silence him. "For you, this may be the 'worse' of 'for better or for worse,'" she said, "but this the way I am."

Lanny stormed out of the house in a huff. After an hour of driving aimlessly through the country, his crumbling vision for a superwoman wife drew him into a time of soul-searching. He began to think about all the ways Dee had fulfilled or exceeded his expectations. She had been a wonderful, accepting friend to him. She was a warm, caring mother, and she was so creative with things like dinner menus and decorating the house. It also occurred to him that he may not be living up to Dee's expectations in some ways, and she wasn't making demands of him.

When he returned to the house, he brought flowers. He apologized to Dee for his lack of acceptance. "I love you just the way you are," he said.

Wise man!

When you met and married your wife, she was the vision of loveliness. She could do no wrong in your eyes, and you committed yourself to love her for a lifetime. As time went on, however, you discovered that she wasn't a perfect woman. In fact, you found some things about her you didn't care for very much: wrinkles, stretch marks, graying hair, a few extra pounds, and the like. Don't insist through your attitude, words, or "lists" that she go back in time and become the woman she was—or the woman you thought she was. Don't try to make her into something she is not. Love her unconditionally, just as she is.

A woman's acceptance of herself hinges on so many things. Seeing herself through your eyes is perhaps the biggest of them. You are her mirror. She sees herself most clearly in how you respond to her. You guard her heart by loving her despite her flaws. You protect her by loving her even if she doesn't change. When she looks at you and sees unconditional love and acceptance shining back at her, she will more readily accept herself. Let her know through your words of affirmation, your supportive prayers, and your positive body language that she is your one and only.

Key 6: Demonstrate Spiritual Leadership

You may not believe it, but the most desirable—if not alluring—quality Christian women find in their men is godliness. Barb and I have heard this from wives all across the country. We hear comments like these, sometimes as a compliment and sometimes as a wish:

- ⊕ "When I get up in the morning, I usually find him reading his Bible or praying at the kitchen table."
- ⊕ "He's the one who gets up early on Sunday morning and makes sure we go to church as a family."
- ⊕ "I so appreciate it when my husband leads the kids and me in family devotions during the week."
- ⊕ "He made all the arrangements for us to attend a

Christian marriage conference last year. He even called my parents to watch the kids."

⊕ "Whenever we're outside with the kids, enjoying the sunset or the flowers, he says things like, 'Thank you, God, for that beautiful sunset.' He helps the kids see that God is real and generous without preaching at them."

You can provide your wife with an enormous amount of security and care by being the spiritual leader God wants you to be in your home. Don't wait until she starts bugging you about leading family devotions or praying with the kids at bedtime. Set the spiritual tone in your home by being a godly man day by day.

Key 7: Pray for Her and with Her

Perhaps the most important expression of your godliness at home is how you pray *for* your wife and *with* your wife. She should be at the top of your prayer list every day. Pray for her safety and her health—physically, emotionally, relationally, and spiritually. Pray for her spiritual growth and witness in her world. Pray for her success in the tasks she undertakes each day. Give her into God's hands, and ask him to use you in being the answer to your prayers for her.

Before you go your separate ways each day, take your wife's hand and pray for her—aloud. Pray about everything she may be involved in that day—her responsibilities, her relationships, her challenges. Ask God to bless her in every way. And before you go to sleep at night, take her hand again and thank God for all he has done in her life.

Before Scott married our daughter Sarah, I took him aside and said, "Scott, you have the opportunity to base your marriage on prayer and spiritual intimacy with Sarah. Start your marriage relationship by loving Sarah as Christ loved the church. Every morning when you wake up or at night right before you go to sleep, take Sarah's hands and pray out loud together. I'm not legalistic. If you miss a day once in a while, it's no big deal. But how about being one of the few guys in America who commits to pray daily with his wife?"

Every so often I check with my son, Scott, to see how he is doing. I am thankful to say that he is on target in this vital area.

As much as Barb and I pray together now, we don't have a stellar long-term record. I didn't start out well in our marriage, but I am hitting the mark now. I'm not perfect, but I am enthusiastic about my role as the servant leader of my home. Your record may not be perfect either. But praying with your wife consistently will draw the two of you together in spiritual intimacy. Nothing will make her feel more safe, secure, and protected than your prayers *for* her and *with* her.

Do you desire to follow through on these seven keys for guarding your wife's heart? Then join me in the following prayer.

> *Dear Father,*
>
> *You know so well who I am—just a man. You know all about my desires, my longings, my insecurities, and my fears. You know, Lord, that I am a man with dreams. I dream of a better life for me, my wife, and my kids.*
>
> *God, please empower me with your own Holy Spirit to guard well the heart of the wife you have placed at my side. I commit myself to being the man she needs me to be, the man you called me to be. I can't do this alone. I need you, and I need the strength of brothers who love you and love me.*
>
> *Forgive me for my sins as a husband, in Jesus' name. Make*

me the kind of man you want me to be, a guardian of my wife, a leader of my family. And I will give you all the glory. Thank you for the privilege of calling you my Father.

Amen.

CAMPAIGN RESOURCES FOR DIVORCE-PROOFING AMERICA'S MARRIAGES

$\mathcal{D}$ear friends,

The resources for the Divorce-Proofing America's Marriages campaign are designed *for you*—to help you divorce-proof your marriage. You and your spouse can certainly read and study these books as a couple. But it's only when you meet with a small group that is committed to divorce-proofing their marriages as well that you'll fully experience the power of these ideas. There's power when believers unite in a common cause. There's power when men and women keep each other accountable. To take on this challenge, you must have a group of friends who are encouraging you every step of the way.

There are several ways you can connect to a small group:

- ⊕ Start your own Divorce-Proofing America's Marriages small group in your church or neighborhood. For workbooks, leader's guides, videos, and other resources for your small group, call 888-ROSBERG (888-767-2374) or visit our Web site at **www.divorceproof.com**.

- ⊕ Give this information to your pastor or elders at your local church. They may want to host a Divorce-Proofing America's Marriages small group in your church.
- ⊕ Call America's Family Coaches at 888-ROSBERG (888-767-2374), or e-mail us at afc@afclive.com and we will connect you with people and churches who are interested in Divorce-Proofing America's Marriages.

Yes, together we can launch a nationwide campaign and see countless homes transformed into covenant homes. But beware. If we do not teach these principles to our own children, we risk missing the greatest opportunity of all: to pass our legacy of godly homes to the next generation. Barb and I believe that, *for the sake of the next generation,* there is no more worthy cause. This holy fire must purify our own homes first.

Gary and Barb Rosberg

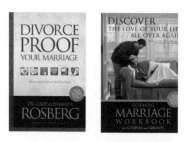

DIVORCE-PROOF YOUR MARRIAGE
ISBN 0-8423-4995-2
Audio CD (3 CDs) ISBN 0-8423-6592-3
Audiocassette (2 cassettes) ISBN 0-8423-6894-9

DISCOVER THE LOVE OF YOUR LIFE ALL OVER AGAIN (workbook)
ISBN 0-8423-7342-X

Your house is weatherproofed. But is your marriage divorce-proofed? In this foundational book of the Divorce-Proofing America's Marriages campaign, Gary and Barb show couples how to keep their marriages safe from the threat of divorce. Divorce doesn't happen suddenly. Over months and years couples can slide from the dream to disappointment and eventually to emotional divorce. However, they can stop the slide by learning to love in six unique ways. Small groups will enjoy the *Discover the Love of Your Life All Over Again* workbook, which includes eight sessions. Together couples will practice healing hurt in their marriages, meeting their spouses' needs, strengthening each other through difficult times, guarding their marriage against threats, celebrating their spouses, and renewing their love for each other day after day. A weekly devotion and assignment will help couples practice what they learn in the context of the encouragement of couples who are committed to the same goal of divorce-proofing their marriages. This workbook includes an easy-to-follow leader's guide.

THE 5 LOVE NEEDS OF MEN AND WOMEN
ISBN 0-8423-4239-7
Audiocassette (2 cassettes) ISBN 0-8423-3587-0

SERVING LOVE (workbook)
ISBN 0-8423-7343-8

You, too, can learn how to become your spouse's best friend with *The Five Love Needs of Men and Women* book and workbook. In this book, Gary talks to women about the deepest needs of their husbands, and Barb talks to men about the most intimate needs of their wives. You'll discover the deep yearnings of your spouse. And when you join a group studying the *Serving Love* workbook, you will learn how to understand and meet your spouse's needs within a circle of encouraging friends. They can help you find ways to meet those needs day after day, week after week. The workbook includes eight group sessions, three weekly activities, and ideas for a date night with your spouse. Easy-to-follow leader's guide included.

GUARD YOUR HEART
ISBN 0-8423-5732-7

GUARDING LOVE (workbook)
ISBN 0-8423-7344-6

We all need to guard our hearts and marriages. It's only in a couples small group, among like-minded friends, that you can get the solid support you need to withstand attacks on your marriage. In *Guard Your Heart,* Gary and Barb Rosberg outline the unique dangers and temptations husbands and wives face. In the *Guarding Love* workbook, the Rosbergs give you the tools to show your small group how to hold each other accountable to guarding their marriages—no matter the cost.

Do you know of a marriage in your church or neighborhood that is vulnerable to attack? Start a small group for that couple with the *Guarding Love* workbook as a resource. Or invite that couple to a small group that is reading and applying this book and workbook. The workbook includes eight exciting group sessions and an easy-to-follow leader's guide.

HEALING THE HURT IN YOUR MARRIAGE: BEYOND CONFLICT TO FORGIVENESS
ISBN 1-58997-104-3   Available Spring 2004

FORGIVING LOVE (workbook)
ISBN 0-8423-7491-4   Available Spring 2004

In *Healing the Hurt in Your Marriage: Beyond Conflict to Forgiveness,* Gary and Barb Rosberg show you how to forgive past hurt in your marriage and close the loop on unresolved conflict. Restore an honest, whole relationship with your spouse. You probably know a dozen marriages that are deteriorating because one spouse is holding a grudge or because the husband and wife have never resolved their conflict, hurt, or anger. And most marriages have past hurts that are hindering the ongoing relationship. Gary and Barb show you how to break free of these past hurts and experience wholeness again. The most effective way to heal wounds is within the circle of encouraging believers who understand, know, and sympathize with you in the common struggles in marriage. The *Forgiving Love* workbook is perfect for small group members who can encourage each other to resolve conflict and start the healing process. Includes eight encouraging sessions and an easy-to-follow leader's guide.

RENEWING YOUR LOVE: DEVOTIONS FOR COUPLES
ISBN 0-8423-7346-2

Have the demands of everyday life pressed in on your marriage? Has your to-do list become more important than your relationship with your spouse? Is the TV the center of your home or the love you and your spouse share? This devotional from America's Family Coaches, Gary and Barb Rosberg, will help you and your spouse focus on your marriage, your relationship, and the love of your life. Let Gary and Barb guide you through thirty days of renewal and recommitment to your marriage by reviewing forgiving love, serving love, persevering love, guarding love, celebrating love, and renewing love through the lens of Scripture, reflection, prayer, and application.

Look for a persevering love book in the future from Gary and Barbara Rosberg and Tyndale House Publishers. This book will help you weather the storms of life without losing the passion for your spouse.

Also watch for a celebrating love book from your favorite family coaches, Gary and Barb Rosberg. This book will give you creative ideas on how to keep the fire and passion alive in your marriage.

Begin to divorce-proof your home, your church, and your community today

Contact your local bookstore that sells Christian books for all of the resources of the Divorce-Proofing America's Marriages campaign

or

call 888-ROSBERG (888-767-2374)

or

visit our Web site at

www.divorceproof.com.

DR. GARY & BARBARA ROSBERG

40 UNFORGETTABLE DATES WITH YOUR MATE

ISBN 0-8423-6106-5

When's the last time you and your spouse went on an unforgettable date? Saying "I do" certainly doesn't mean you're finished working at your marriage. Nobody ever put a tank of gas in a car and expected it to run for years. But lots of couples are running on emotional fumes of long-ago dates. Truth is, if you're not dating your spouse, your relationship is not growing. Bring the zing back into your marriage with *40 Unforgettable Dates with Your Mate,* a book that gives husbands and wives ideas on how they can meet the five love needs of their spouse. Wives, get the inside scoop on your husband. Men, discover what your wife finds irresistible. Gary and Barb Rosberg show you how, step-by-step, in fun and creative dates.

CONNECTING WITH YOUR WIFE
ISBN 0-8423-6020-4

Want to understand your wife better? Barbara Rosberg talks directly to men about what makes women tick. She'll help you understand your wife's emotional wiring as she shows you how to communicate more effectively and connect sexually in a way that's more satisfying to your spouse. She also reveals the single best thing you can do for your marriage—and why it's so important.

CHAPTER 2
1. *Merriam-Webster's Collegiate Dictionary,* 10th ed., s.v. wellspring.

CHAPTER 6
1. Maggie Scarf, *Intimate Partners* (New York: Random House, 1987). See also <www.family.org/pastor/reviews/a0012018.html> for the same statistics.

CHAPTER 11
1. Barbara and Allen Pease, *Why Men Don't Listen and Women Can't Read Maps* (New York: Welcome Rain, 2000), 136.
2. Michelle Weiner-Davis, *A Woman's Guide to Changing Her Man* (New York: Golden Books, 1998), 7.
3. Ibid., 66.
4. Pease, *Why Men Don't Listen and Women Can't Read Maps,* 76.
5. John Gottman with Nan Silver, *Why Marriages Succeed or Fail* (New York: Simon and Schuster, 1994),143–44.
6. Kevin Leman, *Making Sense of the Men in Your Life: What Makes Them Tick, What Ticks You Off, and How to Live in Harmony* (Nashville: Thomas Nelson, 2000), quoted in *Marriage* (March/April 2002): 29–30.

$\mathcal{D}$r. **Gary and Barbara Rosberg** are America's Family Coaches—equipping and encouraging America's families to live and finish life well. Having been married for nearly thirty years, Gary and Barbara have a unique message for couples. The Rosbergs have committed the next decade of their ministry to divorce-proofing America's marriages. The cornerstone book in that campaign is *Divorce-Proof Your Marriage*. Other books the Rosbergs have written together include their bestselling *The Five Love Needs of Men and Women*, *40 Unforgettable Dates with Your Mate*, *Renewing Your Love: Devotions for Couples*, and other books about marriage.

Together Gary and Barbara host a nationally syndicated, daily radio program, *America's Family Coaches . . . LIVE!* On this live call-in program heard in cities all across the country, they coach callers on many family-related issues. The Rosbergs also host a Saturday radio program on the award-winning secular WHO Radio.

The Rosbergs' flagship conference, "Discover the Love of Your Life All Over Again," is bringing the Divorce-Proofing America's Marriages campaign to cities across America. They are on the national speaking teams for FamilyLife "Weekend to Remember" marriage conferences and FamilyLife "I Still Do" arena events for couples. Gary also has spoken to thousands of men at Promise Keepers stadium events annually since 1996 and to parents and adolescents at Focus on the Family "Life on the Edge Tour" events.

Gary, who earned his Ed.D. from Drake University, has been a marriage and family counselor for twenty years. He coaches CrossTrainers, a men's Bible study and accountability group of more than six hundred men.

Barbara, who earned a B.F.A. from Drake University, has written *Connecting with Your Wife* in addition to several other books with Gary. She also speaks to women, coaching and encouraging them by emphasizing their incredible value and worth.

The Rosbergs live outside Des Moines, Iowa, and are the parents of two adult daughters: Missy, a college student studying communications; and Sarah, who lives outside Des Moines with her husband, Scott, and their son, Mason.

For more information on the ministries of
America's Family Coaches, contact:

America's Family Coaches
2540 106th Street, Suite 101
Des Moines, Iowa 50322
1-888-ROSBERG
www.divorceproof.com

Tune In to
America's Family Coaches
. . . LIVE!

Listen every weekday for strong coaching on all your marriage, family, and relationship questions. On this interactive, call-in broadcast, Gary and Barbara Rosberg tackle real-life issues by coaching callers on many of today's hottest topics. Tune in and be encouraged by America's leading family coaches.

For a listing of radio stations broadcasting
America's Family Coaches . . . LIVE!
call 1-888-ROSBERG
or
visit our Web site at www.afclive.com.